C000065229

The History of Some Stuff

Ethan Cox

Copyright © 2021 Ethan Cox

All rights reserved.

ISBN: 9798712554225

THE HISTORY OF SOME STUFF

Dedicated to those who like to know weird facts, as well as all the teachers who've had the most immense strength that I've ever been fortunate enough to witness.

AND
OTHERS
THAT
WORK
AT SCHOOLS

Also a huge thank you to my sister who managed to edit and resolve my dreadful splelling.

Dear R. R.,

Hope you've had an awesome Easter & have an awesome time reading this.

From Ethan Cox.

7/04/2021.

CONTENTS

THE HISTORY OF SOME STUFF

INTRODUCTION

Okay, I get that this book is a bit weird. It has condoms, vodka and houseplants in it. Of course it's going to be a bit weird. But on the plus side, you can now annoy your friends with random facts about random things. That's one of the great joys in life.

This book contains no mention of coronavirus, thank goodness.

So, each chapter is accompanied with a page titled "Other facts that didn't make the cut" and is a page with other random facts concerning the subject of the chapter. Not only that, but each chapter has a relatively comical poem to accompany it. Why? Who knows really, I just started writing a poem for toasters and it sort of went on from there.

This book is fantastic for those that have a dreadful attention span, as you don't even have to read every chapter if you don't want to. You don't have to read them in any particular order; choose your favourites as a starting point and go from there. Obviously, you can read from front to back. That's what I'd do. But there's no way of me enforcing that, so... yeah.

I wrote this book because I get unbelievably bored when I'm not learning something new, and not trying to do new things with my brain. When I find something new, often that's all that I do and all I can think about. In the past, this has included table tennis, chess, calligraphy... I mean just some weird stuff. This has been one of those things for me. When my family bought Trivial Pursuit, I became a little obsessed with really random facts, but I didn't like putting my knowledge of random facts to waste. So, I started to watch shows like The Chase and Tipping Point. But they were too slow. Not enough substance. So, the obvious thing to do was to write a book. So here I am, writing a book, being a self-published author. Little weird if I'm honest. Make my Wikipedia page nice please. Tell them I have six-pack abs.

THE HISTORY OF SOME STUFF

1
TOASTERS

The toaster gets many of us up in the morning. The smell of the burnt breadcrumbs lying at the bottom are to die for. On average, American households spend 35 hours a year feeding 75 million mouths every day in the USA alone. 88% of us consider it a staple in the household kitchen, but it's only been that way since 1924.

Toasting bread has been around for centuries, however. As many things do, it started out with the Egyptians and the Romans. The people of Ancient Greece may have been 'toasting' bread, but their bread didn't have the same kind of allure the smell of a bakery does today. That allure was invented by the Egyptians, but it was soon found out that this glorious invention of bread created a habitable bed for mould (a significant detraction from the allure). First produced in about 3300BC, bread was extremely important to the Egyptians with it being the currency for many workers, such as the workers for the Pyramids of Giza. This meant that poor workers had to find a way to keep this bread for a prolonged period of time. Thus, toasting was born. This was first and most clearly shown in the Old Kingdom tomb of Miankhkhnum and Khnumhotep at Saqqara.

Image Credit: Oxford Expedition to Egypt

These carvings raise two questions: how do you pronounce a word with six consecutive consonants that isn't "rhythm", and what do the carvings show?

Bread had to be mass produced. It's a common misconception that slaves built the pyramids. All of them were paid workers and were paid in bread (very jealous), meaning thousands and thousands of loaves of bread needed to be made every day. This demand needed its supply, so factory-esque chains were set up to make the bread, as seen in the tomb. However, it wasn't only the workers. The big man (or Cleopatra) on top wanted thousands upon thousands of loaves of all different types of bread, whether they were dead or alive. Rameses III was buried with 1,824,043 loaves of bread. Why? Probably food for the afterlife. Or he really wanted to feed the ducks.

The Romans were next to use this idea of toasting, and started toasting their bread from around 500BC. They gave us our word for "toast", coming from the Latin "toastum", meaning "to burn or scorch". It came from a rather strange tradition of putting a small piece of burnt bread into wine. Supposedly, doing so reduced the acidity of the wine, making it slightly more palatable. This gave rise to the

English verb "to toast" — as in, to raise your glass to a person or occasion. After this, they found that eating not-quite-burnt-but-not-quite-raw bread was delicious. Before, putting bread on a hot stone or in front of a fire would be the preferred method of toasting, but devices were made to create a nice and even toast. This era of toast gave rise to one of the first appliances for toasting (besides the hot stone which I don't think really counts as an appliance): frames were created specifically to toast bread. This toast could be used by the armies for a (relatively) good source of nutrition as well as for long distance journeys due to it being both yummy and having anti-mould properties. When the armies of Rome invaded Britain, they took their toast and their toasting method with them.

The idea of a toaster remained largely the same until around 1870 when the invention of the coal stove came along, revolutionising the toasting industry. Admittedly, there wasn't much of an industry, but it meant that wires and frames could be produced by various companies to insert slices of bread and toast them. *Almost* amazing.

This lasted until the early 1900s when electricity started to become commonplace in people's homes. Electricity means appliances, and appliances mean toasters. A couple of years earlier, a Scotsman by the name of Alan MacMasters invented the first ever electrical toaster in 1893, called "Eclipse". As much as I'd love to say this changed the world, it didn't. In fact, it was a failure. Electricity wasn't widespread at the time and it didn't really work. In fact, it led to the first toaster related death in 1894, when a lady in Guildford, UK, found herself in a kitchen engulfed with flames. MacMasters responded to this by blaming the deceased for "not holding appropriate respect for the power of the electric toaster." This was because the wire of the toaster was easily melted. You would've thought they'd have tested it.

It almost all changed when American metallurgist Albert Marsh created an alloy that could withstand the heat in 1905. Nichrome (80% nickel and 20% chromium) was 300 times stronger than its predecessor. Despite this, it took a further three years for the first commercially successful toaster to be released, but it only toasted one side at a time and didn't have the classic pop-up mechanism that makes a toaster a toaster. Finally, in 1921, Charles Strite invented the pop-up toaster. His motivation to create such a device? Receiving burnt toast constantly from his factory cafeteria in Stillwater, Minnesota. After registering the patent, Strite managed to receive financial backing to create the Waters Genter company, managing to sell to restaurants and cafes across the USA.

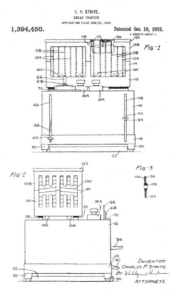

Patent for the first electric toaster, named "Bread Toaster"

In 1926, the Waters Gaters company had yet another

breakthrough when he added a lever to the toaster, allowing the user to choose how toasty they wanted it. It became the go-to wedding present of 1926, fetching around $150 in today's standards. The toaster was aptly named "The Toastmaster".

It was indeed the master of toast.

Commercially, it was a success, and the company's name changed from "Waters Genter" to "Toastmaster, Inc.". Sadly, Strite passed away on the 18th of October 1921, the same day he received his patent, meaning he was unable to live out his success. It was also the day that Ludwig III of Bavaria died. Although I'll admit that's irrelevant.

Nevertheless, Strite's invention made the world a better place, one slice of bread at a time.

The modern-day toaster industry now is massive reaching USD 3.52 billion in 2020. It's expected to reach USD 4.5 billion by 2025. Who knew.

Other facts that didn't quite make the cut:

- The first invention of the toaster controlled by the interned was in 1990.
- On the 19th of February 2002, a toaster sold on eBay for $6,331.
- There's an online toaster exhibition: www.toastermuseum.com.
- Humans have a "toast centre" in their brains, dedicated for smelling burning toast. Why? Because having to eat burnt toast sucks.
- There's a phenomenon called the "buttered toast phenomenon", which is an observation that buttered toast lands butter-side down. It's used as an idiom to represent pessimistic outlooks. There is no correlation between the side toast lands and which side is buttered.
- Toast is mentioned in Shakespeare's "The Merry Wives of Windsor", where Falstaff says, "Go fetch me a quart of sack – put a toast in't."
- French Toast isn't French. The French call it "pain perdu", or lost bread.
- Toast has been part of American *haute cuisine* since the 1850s.
- Wikipedia states that "Avocado toast is seen as a symbol of millennial culture." OK boomer.
- Wikipedia also has an entire page dedicated to dishes containing toast. This includes "Tongue Toast" (toast with scrambled egg and sauteed beef tongue), and "Eggs in the basket" (a favourite for Love Island viewers).
- MacMasters received 227,299 nominations to appear on the new £50 bank note in 2018.

Poem about toast:

Oh, what one would do for toast,

Its outer crust and the innermost

soft bed of deliciousness.

Oh, what one would do for a toaster,

I don't want to be a boaster,

but get rid of suspiciousness,

and clear any unknown by saying

my toaster is superior.

It's able to toast the bagel,

the inside soft yet the edges stable.

Although,

it struggles with large sourdough.

Oh, what one would do for toast.

Me? I'd pay for a toaster.

2
VODKA

For some people, vodka isn't an everyday occurrence. But for some, it is. And the history of it is interesting. So there. It's in the book.

Let me start by saying that I don't condone drinking vodka. A study in 2008 showed that vodka is one of the unhealthiest alcoholic drinks and that the estimates for the annual death toll resulting from vodka consumption extend to the thousands in Russia. It's a lot less everywhere else, but it's still thousands.

As a lot of terrible-things-for-your-body begin, vodka started as a medicine, being prescribed in eastern Europe as a tonic and to cure ailments such as fatigue and various skin ailments in the 16th century. Although, it wasn't like the vodka that we know today, as it had a similar proof to wine, being around 14%. Because of this, and its taste, people referred to it as "burning wine". This name is still used is many northern European countries (*Branntwein* in German, *brandewijn* in Dutch, *brennevin* in Norwegian), but our word for "vodka" comes from the Slavic word "*voda*", meaning "water". Did they drink it as much as water? Probs.

The first mention of the word "vodka" was way back in 1405 in Poland, where it was recorded as a chemical compound for medicines and cosmetics, but it may have been as early as 1386 when Genoese ambassadors first brought vodka to Russia as "*aqua vitae*", or "*the water of life*". Unsurprisingly, the Russians loved it, but still tried to perfect the recipe. Russian orthodox monk Isodore of the Chudov Monastery in Moscow is widely credited for the first recipe for vodka, or as it was known then as "bread wine". Because of the close ties with the Kremlin, the beverage was not allowed outside of Moscow and was produced solely for the Grand Duchy of Moscow. Who knew vodka was so prestigious.

It didn't become common in Russia until Polish merchants brought it to the area of Kievan in 1533. A year later, Stefan Familierz published "*On Herbs and Their Potency*", having the (much contested and not specific at all) title of "the most lavishly illustrated volumes published in Poland in the early sixteenth century." In this, Familierz stated it could increase fertility and awaken lust. I was unaware that getting drunk had such an effect.

From this, vodka was developed. By 1580, the city of Poznań had over 497 distilleries, and Polish vodka dominated the industry, becoming standard in the Netherlands, Denmark, Russia, Austria, Romania, Ukraine and so on. These nations would come to be known as the "vodka belt", a continuous line of countries that all prefer spirits over beer and wine.

In the 18th century, vodka became a massive hit. Regular wine was far more expensive than so-called "burning wine" as "burning wine" could be diluted with water, usually to around 24%. This drink went on to be sold usually to taverns all around Europe. It was around this time when people became very creative with their methods of making vodka, sometimes using carrot and even extracts from milk.

No thank you.

Empress Elizabeth of Russia caused the next major change in the vodka industry. On the 8th of June 1751, a decree was made stating that the ownership of vodka distilleries would be regulated by the Russian government. Because of the way vodka was made, it was inexpensive and relatively easy to produce, meaning the government was missing a trick by not monopolising on it, missing out on massive profits. This created a huge spike in the price of vodka, making it the drink for many Russian elites. It took Alexander II, infamous for chain-smoking and gambling, for everything to change over a century later. In 1863, the policy was repealed, allowing vodka to trickle down to the masses. However, there was still high taxation on vodka, which was fundamental in funding the government, with vodka accounting for 40% of state revenue. Let me repeat that: 40% of all money that the Russian government received was from vodka. By the start of WWI, vodka comprised 89% of all alcohol consumed in all of Russia. Poland saw this and realised what a fantastic idea it was. By 1925, Poland had monopolised production and distribution of vodka, a fantastic post-war way to celebrate.

The Russians are the winners for post-war celebrations however, as they drank themselves dry. They partied too hard. After the German surrender on the 9th of May 1945 at 1am, Russians ran out in their pyjamas onto the streets and began to party, and party hard. They went non-stop for 22 hours, drinking a heck-ton of vodka. So much that the entire country ran out of vodka in those 22 hours. A Redditor recounted a story of his grandfather and his celebrations that day, and what happened the day after. He said that "The only day I was ever blackout drunk was the 9th of May 1945. I woke up on the street hugging two loaves of bread." Who doesn't.

A household name of vodka in Russia, the USA and the UK is Smirnoff, founded in 1864, just one year after Alexander II repealed the decree. It was founded by Pyotr

Smirnov, and his vodka became one of the Tsar's favourites. But during the Russian Revolution in 1917, the Smirnov family was forced to flee with Pyotr's third son, Vladimir Smirnov, taking the reins and establishing a factory in 1920 in Constantinople (modern day Istanbul). However, before this, Vladimir became a rebel of the Russians, joining the anti-Bolshevik White Army and helping many refugees escape Russia via the south. Soon after, Russian forces managed to locate him, ambush him, and sentence him to death via firing squad. Luckily, the White Army liberated the camp and he was free. Well, almost. He fled to Crimea where he was shipped across the Black Sea, and then finally into Constantinople. How is this not a movie.

After another move from Constantinople to France, Vladimir moved to America, where Smirnoff is still made to this day.

That isn't the only controversy involving vodka, however. Sweden has been central in a vodka-controversy, with a large proportion of the Swedish black market comprising vodka. So-called "vodka cars" are used by criminals, used to distribute thousands of litres of vodka to people unable to buy it, with some being younger than 13. However, black-market vodka isn't limited to Sweden, with many people producing "bathtub vodka" in Russia that has a proof of 95%. Yikes.

There was also a Vodka War, which had to have been named by drama queens. Apparently, there were "heated discussions" within the EU about the definition of vodka, as Cîroc was branded as vodka, despite being made exclusively from grapes. Polish MEP Ryszard Czarnecki stated "Would the French like champagne to be distilled from plums, and would the British accept whisky from apricots? That sounds like heresy." Big words. As a result, the EU stated that vodka needs to be made exclusively from cereals, potatoes and/or sugar beet molasses, and the label for vodka needs to have "Vodka produced from …" on it. I don't know if I'd call that a war. Almost though.

Other facts that didn't make the cut:

- According to www.vodkafacts.net, vodka can increase your lifespan and prevent Alzheimer's. Hmm.
- Vodka goes off after 12 months.
- The EU demands a minimum of 37.5% alcohol content for a beverage to be considered vodka, while the USA demands 40%.
- A quarter of Russian men die before they reach 50, largely because of vodka.
- In the Czech Republic, it's an Easter tradition to spank unmarried women. The young men who do this then go into their house, and the women's father gives them a shot of vodka as a thank you.
- You can buy spicy vodka, some batches reaching 250,000 Scoville (AKA very hot).
- Soviets drank half a glass of vodka every two hours in Chernobyl, supposedly to clear the thyroid gland of radiation.
- A shot of vodka contains only 70 calories. Bring it on.
- There's a myth that Dimitri Mendeleev created the first standard 40% proof vodka.
- A 2011 WHO report found that annual alcohol consumption in Russia was 15.76 litres per capita.

Poem about vodka:

One shot, two shot, three shot, four,

I've had too much but I'll have some more.

It's made from potatoes; it's made from rye.

Whatever you do, don't put it in your eye.

Five shot, six shot, seven shot, eight,

I'll be honest, it's getting quite late.

Yet here I am, still drinking away.

Oh my gosh, am I wasted today.

And, I know, I'll wake up tomorrow,

quite hungover and filled with sorrow.

3
BEDS

Something we definitely use every day is a bed. In fact, we use our bed for a third of our lives, unless you're an A-level student, where you'll either be in bed 95% of the time, or 5% of the time. Curiosity about the bed struck me when I was going through a funk, not knowing what to write about, so I lay down. Then it hit me; I knew nothing about beds. So, without further ado: beds.

It's no surprise that the Egyptians were the first to do the bed well, but there are many instances of beds before them. In August 2020, historians discovered what's believed to be grass bedding from at least 200,000 years ago in the Lebombo Mountains of South Africa. It was made of plant material combined with ash, most likely as an insect repellent.

Is it a stretch to say that this rock is a bed? Potentially, but it makes sense considering its location (a cave by a very sheer drop which has a very nice view) and what it's made of (not rocks, so it's more comfortable. Needs little explaining). This was a momentous discovery, as the second oldest bed was 123,000 years younger, also found in South Africa, and looks equally as comfortable. It looks like a rock.

This bed would've been just under the size of a double bed: it was 22 square feet and 12 inches thick. This would've been ideal for hunters grouping together or for families and consists of similar materials (leaves, grass etc.). Seeing these makes me more grateful for my bed.

The ones that really made beds take off were the Egyptians. Rich Egyptians had decorative furniture all over their homes with artistic and intricate designs, all designed with expert craftsmanship. Beds in Egypt were made of wood, however, a rare commodity for the average Egyptian. Nonetheless, the Pharaohs loved them and would have multiple in one tomb. They varied in size and shape, with some sloping up where the headboard and footboard would be nowadays, making a sort of hammock. Their version of pillows sounds strangely nice and horrible at the same time. They were small semi-cylindrical structures that stood on a platform, usually made out of wood. It's said that these are possibly just for those in tombs because of how dreadfully uncomfortable they would be, and because they would be supporting the owner in death.

A "pillow" in Ancient Egypt.

The Romans loved the crap out of beds — especially the rich. They had mattresses stuffed with reeds, hay or wool, and had actual cushions. Wow.

They loved beds so much that they had five types of beds for 5 different types of activities:

- lectus cubularis – normal bed for sleeping
- lectus genialis – the marriage bed
- lectus lucubratorius – the bed for studying (I want it)
- lectus discubitorius – the bed for eating at
- lectus funebris – the death bed

Personally, I think we should bring these back into the 21st century.

It's the same in the Middle Ages really, with the rich having large, decorative beds, and the poor having no beds, or having some straw if they were lucky. The 14th and 15th century were big however, with the middle class becoming wealthier in Europe, and it became standard to have a bed, with many having curtains to keep in the heat in poorly heated homes. These became fashionable and are the reason why lavish beds have curtains. It was also around this time that the Great Bed of Ware was build, known for its size (3.38m x 3.26m) and extravagancy for its time. It's referenced in no less than 9 books, including Shakespeare's *Twelfth Night*. It is now on display at the V&A in London.

Fast forward to the "Century of Magnificent Beds", or better known as the 17th century. With the arrival of Louis XIV in France arrived wealth and extravagancy. He had 413 beds in his palaces (really good for hide and seek), with most having the most decorative decadent features. In his main bed in Versailles, it's said that there's so much gold surrounding and on his bed that the velvet can hardly be seen. The people of France looked up to this uselessness of wealth and decided they wanted a piece of it as well. Beds became standard for the wealthy, the average and the poor.

I think beds have gone downhill since the 1600s. Nonetheless, Wikipedia currently lists no less than 34 types of bed, including the rather progressive cabinet bed, not for its design but by who designed it.

Sarah Elisabeth Goode was born 1855 in Toledo, Ohio. After being born into slavery, she was granted her freedom after the American Civil war and opened her own furniture store and started inventing. She came up with the cabinet bed, ideal for small spaces that looked like a desk when not folded down. She was granted the patent on the 14th of July 1885 and was the first African American woman to receive a US patent. This was a hit in New York City, where spaces were tight, and people needed space-solutions. She also patented the Murphy bed, which is still used commonly to this day. You can see the patent for the cabinet bed here:

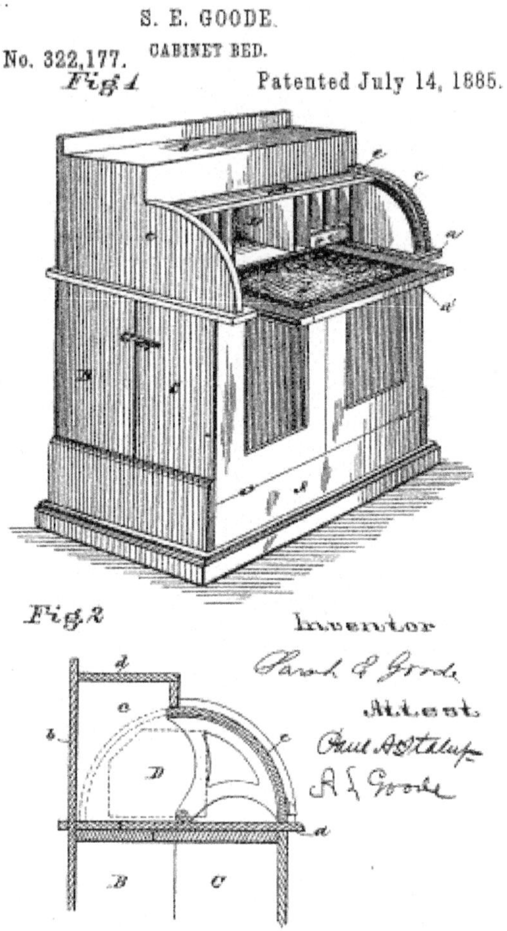

S. E. GOODE.
CABINET BED.
No. 322,177.
Fig 1
Patented July 14, 1885.

Fig 2

Inventor

Sarah E. Goode

Attest

All in all, beds in history have been revolutionary. Well, kind of. They still help us sleep. That's the conclusion.

Other facts that didn't make the cut:

- The most expensive bed in the world is the Baldacchino Supreme Bed, worth USD 6.3 million.
- As of when this book is being written, Wikipedia sates that a bed is "a piece of furniture which is used as a place to sleep, relax, or engage in sexual activities."
- Pillows were once a threat to masculinity, so men used logs as cushions and pillows.
- The biggest bed in the world was made in the Netherlands in 2011, measuring 53ft 11in x 86ft 11in. Comfy.
- The fitted sheet was only invented in 1958.
- The phrase "sleep tight" comes from ropes being tied around the mattresses, so it didn't sag.
- 43% of children from the ages three to four years' old have a television in their bedroom. I also want this.
- Humans can survive longer without food than they can without sleep.
- Giraffes sleep for 1.9 hours per day in 10-minute stints. Me currently.
- Koalas sleep for 22 hours a day. What I want to be.
- No one really knows why we sleep. It doesn't conserve energy as our brain is so active in our sleep and saves the same amount of energy as a KitKat bar.

Poem about beds:

Bed, bed, bed, bed.

Makes me happy and fills with dread.

Oh, how it is so very comfy,

but I have to leave it and so, I'm grumpy.

Bed, bed, bed, bed.

It's got crumbs in it, and now I'm dead.

That's going to make mum upset.

Breakfast in bed? Such regret.

Bed, bed, bed, bed.

I should not have had that bread.

Now, I have to get up in the night,

unless I make my bum hole tight.

Bed, bed, bed, bed.

Makes me happy and fills with dread.

4
CONDOMS

What better next to talk about than condoms after beds. They work perfectly together. Well, most of the time. Condoms only have a 98% success rate with *perfect use*. But let's pretend that everyone from the ages of 18 to 21 uses condoms perfectly. Now, the average couple in that age range has sex 112 times a year. I'm just going off numbers, but to me, that's a baby. Two babies if you're unlucky. But historically, this isn't that bad considering what condoms used to be made of.

The first condom in history is on a French cave wall (romantic) and is a drawing of a man with some sort of skin of an animal over his member. 15,000 years ago, this man didn't want to have a baby. Weirdly, this goes against every evolutionary instinct that men have, but in some way, having a condom would have benefitted him. There's the potential that this was worn ritually, but it's more fun to think that he didn't want an unplanned pregnancy.

A few thousand years later, the Egyptians found out about condoms, but used it less for sex and more for other reasons. They used loincloths to protect their penises from the sun (what!) and to protect them from injury (what!). It's speculated that men would also wrap these sheets around their penis during sex to protect from insect bites, but I can't see this being true. Surely you'd just move location if there are a bunch of bugs around. Anyway.

Condoms appear in Greek mythology too. King Minos of Crete possessed a Cretan Bull, a magnificent specimen that people would die for. He was supposed to sacrifice it to Poseidon but became greedy and kept it for himself. Poseidon was outraged when he found a large white bull in the sea rather than the Cretan Bull, and cursed his wife, Pasiphae, for having intense love for the Cretan Bull. This is illegal now, but it wasn't back in the day. The infidelity charm was also placed on Minos, meaning that instead of semen, he would ejaculate serpents and scorpions, ultimately killing a multiple of his mistresses after having sex with him (this is up on my list on ways I don't want to die). Not wanting to kill his wife, King Minos would insert the bladder of a goat into Pasiphae, acting as a receptacle for his semen. I have no idea how he finished sex with a penis still attached to his body, but this is the first time that condoms were used as contraception.

The next recorded use of the condom was 2000 years later around 1000 BC on the other side of the world in Asia. The Japanese and Chinese upper class were the ones who used condoms as birth control. They made special condoms called glans condoms, which covered only the head of the penis. They were often decorative and showed wealth — a desirable characteristic — and were often made with silk, animal horns (ouch) and turtle shells (ouch).

Everything speeds up if the Romans did something as they invaded basically everywhere, meaning that there were loads of people that started doing as the Romans do, but there's no record of the Romans using condoms. This means that there's a 2500-year gap in condom history, with the 15th and 16th century being a big year for condoms. With the arrival of French troops everywhere, flirting was everywhere as well, meaning STIs were becoming rampant throughout Europe. This was until Italian Gabriele Falloppio, the same man that discovered the Fallopian tubes, wrote a book called "The French Disease" (no one really liked the French because they gave everyone syphilis). At this time, syphilis was deadly, leaving the person with pustules all over their body, and leaving them dead after a few months. To prevent this, Falloppio suggested a linen sheath soaked in a chemical solution to be dried, covering the glands of the penis and tied to it via a ribbon. He tested this device on 1100 men, and found that none of them had contracted syphilis. Woohoo. Condom popularity increased when syphilis took over Europe and spread towards Asia, but not everyone was a fan. The early 18th century was the time of the anti-condomists. John Campbell, 9th Duke of Argyll, stated in Parliament (unsuccessfully) that condoms should be illegal in 1708, followed by Daniel Turner, condemning the condom in 1717, stating they didn't offer full protection from syphilis (how banning condoms would help, I don't know). He also argued that the condom *promotes* unsafe sex, because the cloth causes a loss of sensation, meaning men would stay away from the condom in any case.

Despite this, no alternative for protection from syphilis was found, and the condom market grew rapidly over the 18th century. Most of the time, they were made from animal skin (usually internal stuff like bladder "skin" or intestines), treated with sulphur to make it softer. Not only that, but they were being sold everywhere, from barber shops to open-air markets all over Europe. However, they were still dreadfully uncomfortable, and so were only worn by the middle and upper class.

This was until 1855, with vulcanised rubber becoming all the rage, and the first rubber condom was produced. By the end of the decade, there were multiple factories mass producing rubber condoms. Not only were they more comfortable, but reusable. Eww. These still only covered the penis glands, but they were becoming more and more popular. People went to the doctors to have medical fittings for more comfortable condoms and to prevent them from falling off. This gave rise to the full-length one-size-fits-all condom that we all know and love. There was still a huge taboo around condoms and sex. Abstinence was taught as the only way to prevent contracting an STI in schools until the 20th century. It got so bad that those who contracted syphilis were denied from many hospitals, as many in the medical community viewed those with STIs as punishment for promiscuity.

War and soldiers seems to be a common theme with condoms, specifically with them contracting STIs. This takes us to the 1900s, and the outbreak of WWI also resulted in the outbreak of syphilis and gonorrhoea. By the end of it, 400,000 cases of syphilis and gonorrhoea had been documented; this was unprecedented territory, and not in a good way. This caused the courts of America to allow condoms to be sold to the public for the first time in 45 years in 1918. Laws were put in place to make sure the quality was decent, and condom sales doubled in the 1920s. It was the roaring 20s after all. This was not the case in France however, as condoms were banned due to falling birth rates.

Latex was the next big thing. Invented in 1920, latex was the chosen material for Youngs Rubber Company. Latex condoms were far easier to produce than their predecessors, being stronger, thinner, and offering a better sensation. The ease of making them allowed the Youngs Rubber Company to become Durex in 1929, the name coming from three key selling points: durability, reliability and excellence. All of these condoms were still hand dipped and therefore, very expensive. One thing was missing: mass production.

The first patent for an automatic condom-making machine was in 1930, worth $20,000, or $2 million nowadays. This meant that condoms could be mass produced and could be sold for a cheap price. Oh yea.

World War II struck, and this was big news for

condoms. They were distributed to all men in the US military, as well as making *all* members of the military watch and look at food, posters and lectures filled with propaganda, making thousands of Americans convert to abstinence, but also increasing the sales of condoms. The war also gave rise to rubber shortages. One might think this was the end of condoms for the war, but condom manufacturing went unrestricted. This meant that condoms were not being used for their desired purpose, such as covering the muzzles of rifle barrels, preventing fouling, and covering corrosive material to protect it. Now, condoms have a bunch of uses that are entirely non-sexual, including covering microphones for underwater scenes, and road waterproofing. Thousands of condoms each year are put into the roads of India in order to increase their resistance to the torrential rain they receive. In fact, only a quarter of condoms in India are used for sexual purposes.

The 60s and 70s were the years when condoms became what they are today. Restrictions tightened as the FDA started to regulate them, and quality testing was more rigid, with them being filled up with air and water as well as being "electrocuted" to find any holes. Heck. Condoms and advertisements for them became legal in Ireland. This was just in time, as the AIDS epidemic arrived in the early 1980s. Condoms were literal life savers, and national condom promotion campaigns could be found across the western hemisphere.

Condoms have become so big now (haha) that they're in prisons all around the world, and their use is only expected to grow. The global condom market in 2020 was valued at USD 9.2 billion. That's more than toasters.

Other facts that didn't make the cut:

- For no reason at all, Wikipedia has a picture titled "*A Used Condom on the Street*".
- Japan uses the most condoms.
- There are spray-on condoms, but they didn't achieve commercial success, as the time it took and the noise it made "killed the mood".
- Bill Gates offered $100,000 grants for people that designed a condom that "significantly preserves or enhances pleasure". Eleven teams received the money.
- France holds the world record for the world's largest condom. It is 72ft, covering the Obelisque in Place de la Concorde for World AIDS Day.
- According to www.indiatimes.com, "The British are still embarrassed to buy condoms."
- However, the UK purchases over 160 million condoms every year.
- Condoms make sex 10,000 times safer.
- Trojan had the first condom advert.
- People that didn't wear condoms during WWII were referred to as "boobs" by propaganda.
- On Valentine's Day in the USA, 87 condoms are sold per second.
- It's a myth that if you wear two condoms at the same time, it's less safe.
- Condoms can hold a gallon of water.
- 42 condoms were given to each athlete in the Sochi Winter Olympic Games in 2014
- Condoms remain effective for about four years.
- Www.therichest.com states that women are "just as likely to receive *organisms*". Not the best gift.

Haiku about condoms:

Yes! Protected sex.

Can't wait for organisms.

This will be pleasant.

5
TOILETS

Take a guess where I got the idea to write about this.

The toilet. Lavatory. Facilities. Privy. Outhouse. Latrine. Whatever you want to call it, you use it every day. Most people do a number one six or seven times a day, with the average person doing a number two, three times a day. Is it just me or is that a lot?

Our story starts in Scotland of all places, with one of the first toilets being used in the islands of Orkney. Admittedly, it was a glorified hole in the floor, but that's what a lot of these toilets are going to be. This was in 3000 BC: the millennium for the latrine. They were popping up all over the world; modern-day Pakistan, Persia, and Mesopotamia.

The Greeks were the first to do it properly, with some places even having plumbing systems, such as the Minoans from Crete (probably because of all the serpents and scorpions from the King's ejaculate). They were the first civilisation to use underground plumbing for washing away sewage in as early as 2700 BC. Crete has very steep cliffs, allowing sewage canals to be built with ease, as gravity was on their side. The population grew, and so did the intricacy of the plumbing systems. This gave rise to what may be the first ever flushing toilet, in the Palace of Knossos. No, there was no lever, but conduits were built into the walls, which allowed water to come down from cisterns and flush away any waste. Grecian architecture at its finest.

Again, as the population grew and people became wealthier, flushing toilets were popping up everywhere, even in public toilets. However, there was a huge divide between the "haves" and the "have-nots", with only the "haves" allowed into public toilets that flushed. These toilets were very decadent and were made of marble and limestone. Everyone would sit in a line, do their thing, and water beneath them would wash it away. Privacy was obviously not their main concern as there were no cubicles. Not only that, but you had to use small stones to wipe. I'll hold it in, thanks.

A thousand years later, the Romans did a similar thing. Their toilets were long wooden benches with small holes cut into them above flowing water, suspiciously similar to the Greeks. The main difference was in the way they wiped: a communal stick was used that had a sponge on the end which was kept in saltwater and vinegar. *Everyone* used it. Aaaaah.

The pipes of Rome and much of the Roman Empire were made of lead. Lead on the periodic table is *Pb,* standing for *Plumbum,* the Latin word for lead. This is the reason we have words such as "plumber" in the English language today.

Despite the pipes and the intricate plumbing, the at-home toilet was a thing of the future. People used a simple bucket to urinate and defecate in, far more useful than having the urine being washed away. The Romans used urine for everything, even washing their clothes. Quite smart too, as urine contains ammonia that gets rid of stains. Can't imagine it smelling the best though.

Toilets didn't change much for a while, but they became more popular and people started using them in their homes, although it was still only something the rich had access to. The toilet would be located far away from the bedroom, so the smell didn't disrupt sleep, but it was close to fireplace or kitchen to keep it warm. Wouldn't want to have a poo in the cold, would we.

The poorer used chamber pots — a portable toilet — derived from the French word *chambre*, which were highly decorative. Historians could identify the century from the decoration. Chamber pots were used all around the world, from the pilgrims in England to the population of Japan. There's an old folk song encouraging people to look in their chamber pots before sitting down, called "The Crabfish", from around 1620. The storyline consists of a man bringing home a lobster for his wife, and not knowing where to put it, he puts it in the chamber pot. Then, in the night, the wife has to poo, and the lobster grabs onto her genitals, causing the husband to freak out. In the state of panic, he gets bitten by the lobster too. It contains very coarse language, and I highly recommend looking it up.

Anyway, back to toilets.

By the 16th century in Europe, things were heating up. Cesspits were being built to collect the population's waste, with streets having gutters to collect the waste thrown out of the windows. This gave rise to the fantastic job of "gong farmers". These poor people would clear out the cesspits, earning sixpence a day (not a bad wage in the 1500s), but went up to their necks in "human ordure", and having the worst working hours, from 9pm to 5am. The faeces would be sold by the gong farmers as "nightsoil" (very nice way of putting it) and was used as fertilizer.

Toilets remained largely the same until the invention of the water closet (where we get "WC" from), paving the way for the modern toilet. Alexander Cumming's patent shows how it works very simply:

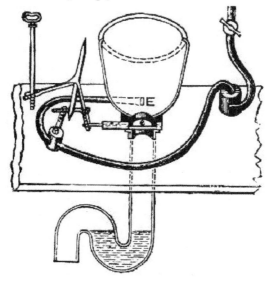

A fantastic invention, revolutionising how we go to the loo. This was ideal for those that wanted to commercialise toilets as well, as it had not really been done before. Enter: *Thomas Crapper*. Arguably the best fact in the book, and or the world, Thomas Crapper revolutionised the toilet. This *is* where we get the word "crap" from. His work can still be seen to this day in Westminster Abbey, London, where manhole covers bear his company name, "Thomas Crapper & Company": an organisation still operating in London that sells some of the most decorative toilets and cisterns you'll ever see, all proudly bearing Crapper's name. Inspirational.

Toilets are pretty much the same since them, although they're going places. Toilets in Japan (fantastic Wikipedia page by the way) are fascinating, many containing games involving aiming, giving you results about your level of control and pressure. Many are connected to the internet and can listen to voice commands. How much is a ticket to Japan…

It would be wrong to not have some notable mentions about deaths on the loo:

- Duke Jing of Jin (say that 10 times fast) died after falling into a toilet pit in 581 BC.
- Edmund II of England may have been assassinated by stabbing on the loo in 1016, the same way Japanese warlord Uesugi Kenshin died in 1578
- Wenceslaus III of Bohemia died when he sat on a spear in the loo.
- Catherine the Great died "whilst attending chamber business".
- Yes, Elvis did die on the loo.
- Judy Garland also died on the loo.

There we go, that's the history of the latrine. Please email me this if you read this on the loo, not for any reason other than I'd find it mildly amusing.

Other facts that didn't make the cut:

- In Afghanistan, there are more TVs than toilets
- 40,000 Americans are injured by toilets every year.
- 26 litres of water are used every time you flush.
- The Chinese have dog toilets.
- 20% of people do not wash their hands after going to the toilet.
- NASA spent $23.4 million on designing a suction toilet.
- Your smartphone has 20 times more bacteria than a toilet handle.
- Great Britain has the most public toilets in the world. They were also voted the worst.
- In medieval times, people used cloves when it smelt bad in the toilet.
- 90% of medicine is excreted through urine.
- Toilet life expectancy is around 50 years.
- Men take more time in the toilet than women.
- The movie *Psycho*, directed by Alfred Hitchcock, caused controversy as it had a flushing toilet. Controversial.
- Toilets have allegedly added 20 years to the average human lifespan.
- $100,000 was spent trying to find whether people prefer toilet paper over the top or under. 75% prefer over.
- It took until WWI for it to be mandatory for public buildings to have toilets.
- Physicians during the Great Plague recommended drinking urine.

Limerick about toilets:

Oh, what to do without a latrine.

Times would be rough, with a lot to clean.

Crap out on the streets

with the people you meet,

and no flush; you'd be more green.

6
DONUTS

Ah, yes. The simple donut. Possibly one of my favourite foods, and probably one of the unhealthiest. Despite this, I still eat many of them. Nom nom nom.

It's possible that donuts have been around since medieval times, with the Arabs frying small pieces of yeasted dough and covering them with sugar syrup, circa the 12th or 13th century (these small pieces of fried dough would evolve Arabia and Greece to become what are now known as *lokma*. These are pastries made of deep-fried dough that are eaten at times of religious importance, such as Hanukkah, Epiphany and Ramadan. The word *lokma* comes from the Arabic word *luqma*, meaning *morsel*).

It didn't take long for travellers to taste small pieces of fried dough and find them absolutely sublime, taking them back to Europe where the Dutch had a field day. They called them *olykoeks*, meaning "oil cake", and loved them so much that the settlers took them wherever they went, including New Amsterdam, or modern-day New York. In 1615, the Dutch landed in America, with settlers arriving in New Amsterdam in 1624. From here on out, donuts would be seen as an American food. These were still not the donuts that we know and love today, however. It took until 1847 for Hanson Gregory, a 16-year-old American to make the hole in the donut. The lime-trader was frustrated with how greasy the donuts were, and the centre of them was often undercooked or raw. Blech. His solution for this? Use the ship's tin pepper box to punch out the hole of the donut. His mother went on to say that he "made a wicked deep-fired dough that cleverly used her son's spice cargo of nutmeg and cinnamon, along with lemon rind", and "put hazelnuts or walnuts in the venter, where the dough might not cook through." Sounds like a donut to me.

This wasn't the only thing that the Dutch did with this idea, though. When they settled in South Africa in March 1647, a whole new culture was formed: Afrikaans.

Koeksisters have been around since the 17th century, with no danger of dying out. The name comes from the Dutch *koek*, meaning cake, and the word *sister* coming from a legend of two sisters that worked together, spending their days plaiting donuts and dunking them in syrup (although some claim that *sis* comes from the sound the dough makes when frying in the oil). Although originally using pasta dough, current koeksisters are made using a dough that is similar to that used in donuts, and they're absolutely delicious (not that I'm at all biased). South Africans love koeksisters so much that there's even a sculpture of a koeksister in Orania, Northern Cape, standing over two metres tall.

Donuts were involved in WWI as well, giving us what is now known as National Donut Day, celebrated on the first Friday of every June, mainly in America (surprise). This is all thanks to the Salvation Army, who sent 250 volunteers to France in the warm providing freshly baked goods from huts in abandoned buildings. They were an instant hit in the midst of war and the volunteers often made up to 300 donuts and over 700 cups of coffee a day. These women became known as either "Donut Girls" or "Donut Dollies".

This should be a movie.

An advertisement for Donut Dollies in 1918

However, this isn't the only Donut Day in America. It's The 10th of November 1970s, and you're an American stuck in the Son Tay prison camp in Vietnam. You're tired. You're hungry. You and your mates come up with a scheme. A scheme so devilish that you create a national holiday (kind of). You convince the prison guards in Son Tay prison camp that it's National Donut Day. You see a glimmer of sympathy in their eyes. They leave, coming back hours later with donuts.

Yes, this is a true story. This should also be a movie.

This made the second National Donut Day, celebrated on the 5th of November in America.

Writing this chapter gave me what I call "extreme cravings". Most people might call it this as well, and you may also be experiencing such cravings. For that, I apologise, but you should really go buy some. For me as well.

Other facts that didn't make the cut:

- Donuts are sold in McDonalds in Denmark.
- 10 billion donuts are made in the USA each year.
- 10 people in the USA have the last name "Donut".
- A chocolate glazed donut contains five teaspoons of sugar.
- Admiral Richard E. Byrd took 100 barrels of donut flour with him on his expedition to the South Pole.
- Researchers have found that the size of a country's donut hole correlates with the quality of its economy.
- The French used to call donuts *Pet de Nonne*, meaning "Nun's farts".
- The record for the most donuts eaten in three minutes is only six. Sounds doable, no?
- The first automatic donut machine was invented in 1920, by Adolph Levitt.
- Renee Zellweger allegedly ate 20 donuts a day to go from a size six to a size 14 in three months for her appearance as Bridget Jones.
- Donuts are 25% fat. Yum.
- The largest box of donuts contained 2,700 donuts.
- German-Americans eat jelly-filled donuts on New Year as it brings good luck.
- The largest donut mosaic contained 7,040 donuts. It was in Ukraine and pictured a *pampukh*, a symbol of Christmas.

Poem about donuts:

Holes in the middle,

or filled like a pie.

There's many ways to have them,

but eat too many, you'll die.

Covered in sugar,

covered in salt.

Have another one,

It's not your fault.

They're just too nice,

you can't step away.

They're just too scrumptious,

but check how much you weigh.

Holes in the middle,

filled like a pie.

There's many ways to have them,

but eat too many, you'll die.

7
CHEWING GUM

Chewing gum, AKA every teacher's nemesis for no reason. Gum is sold everywhere around the world (besides Singapore, where it's banned and you can only get it if you have a prescription, but they don't count in this), but it took its time before being in the limelight.

There's a handful of evidence that the Mayans and the Aztecs were the first to chew gum, circa 3000 BC, but gum was used in various ancient civilisations at the same time, with not one single point of origin. Anyway, the Mayans and the Aztecs chewed on *chicle*, a natural tree gum that is still used in some gum production to this day. Why did they chew it? Well, three reasons: it would clean teeth, it would stave off hunger and every human has the instinctual desire to masticate (sounds like a naughty word but isn't).

As mentioned before, the Mayans and the Aztecs weren't the only ones. The Greeks did it as well, chewing on mastic gum, made from the resin of the mastic trees. These are also called *tears of Chios*, as they were grown on the island of Chios, and are shaped more or less like teardrops. This is also where we get our word for masticate (again, not naughty). These tears of Chios grew into the culture of Chios, so much so that during its Ottoman reign, mastic gum was worth the same as gold, and the penalty for stealing it was execution by order of the sultan (dun dun duuun).

Getting side-tracked. Back to ancient history.

People on (almost) every continent had a means of chewing:

- The Chinese chewed on Ginseng plant root (very healthy)
- The American settlers chewed on tobacco (less healthy)
- The Inuits chewed on blubber
- The South Americans chewed on coca leaves
- The South Asians chewed on betel nuts
- The West Africans chewed on kola nuts

However, the gum that changed it all was chewed by the Native Americans, who chewed the resin made from the sap of spruce trees. It took until 1848 for this to be commercialised; John B. Curtis, a New England settler, saw what the natives were doing and loved it. So much so that he made a product, called "The State of Maine Pure Spruce Gum". Rolls off the tongue.

The State of Maine Pure Spruce Gum was revolutionary for the settlers, and it was a great commercial success. It got so big, that he set up a company (Curtis & Son) and employed 200 people in a three-storey building. He got this money from being a travelling salesman and has earnt the title of "The First Commercial Sales Broker as a Representative of an Eastern Business Marketing Firm". (Disclaimer: this is not an official award. He's just believed to be the first one to do something like this). Curtis was the inventor of all the machinery that made the gum, but never patented any of it. Despite this, he still came up with nine flavours of gum, and earned modern-day millions. He bequeathed his funds to a town named Bradford, Maine, for a new library. The library, aptly named the John B. Curtis Free Public Library, stands to this day, and is listed on the National Register of Historic Places. What a cool dude.

This led to the first flavoured gum being invented in the 1860s by the Kentucky-based pharmacist, John Colgan. He flavoured his gum with powdered sugar and tolu, a powder made from the balsam tree, and is said to be extremely aromatic, which he originally used in cough syrup. This made his small sticks of "Taffy Tolu".

Advertisement for "Taffy Tolu", manufactured by Colgan.

He also used chicle but made it very easy for himself by inventing the "Chewing Gum Chip Forming Machine", patented on the 2nd of August 1910. This automatically cut chips of chewing gum from larger chips. He didn't stop here though, and patented the "Web-cutting Attachment for Wrapping Machines" to cut wrappers for his chewing gum. His company, Colgan Chewing Gum Company, was a huge success, and sold out the following year.

Modern chewing gum, however, was brought to America by none other than the former President of

Mexico, Antonio Lopez de Santa Anna, who thought it would be a suitable replacement for tires. It was not. In fact, it worked so well as gum than Thomas Adams, an entrepreneur, founded the company Chiclets, a gum company which still manufactures gum in Mexico. Adams patented a chewing gum machine in 1871. Because of this mass production, Adams seemingly had a monopoly on the market. This was until Wrigley's.

All credit to Wrigley's for its success. The founder, William Wrigley Jr. had been at it for a long time, trying to commercialise all sorts of things, one of them being baking powder. Unfortunately, the baking powder business wasn't doing so great, so he started making chewing gum, so he could give away two free sticks of chewing gum with each purchase of baking powder as an incentive to buy. Wrigley found that his incentive was more popular than his actual product and went into business from there. Wrigley took a risk and mortgaged everything he owned and put the money into advertising. He was not expecting the fame that enveloped him, as his adverts and gum became a national name. By the time of his death, he was worth \$34 million, approximately \$646,431,824 in today's money. Heck, that's a lot of money.

That's where chewing gum is today. 187 billion hours' worth of gum will be chewed this year. For something you can't even swallow, is it worth it? Well, the chewing gum industry in 2019 was valued at over \$32 billion. That's a lot. A lot more than toasters.

Other facts that didn't make the cut:

- Chewing gum is the world's most common habit.
- 35% of all chewing gum is made by the Wrigley Company.
- Every year, over 373 trillion sticks of chewing gum are produced.
- Over 100,000 tonnes of chewing gum will be chewed each year
- Chewing gum increases blood flow to the brain.
- Chewing gum burns about 11 calories an hour.
- If you swallow gum, it won't stay in your digestive tract for seven years.
- The average person chews 300 sticks of gum per year.
- If you chew gum when chopping onions, you won't cry.
- Www.chewinggumfacts.com lists 13 types of chewing gum. I'd lose that bet.
- 44 pieces of chewing gum are eaten per second in the USA alone.
- The largest piece of chewing gum was the same size as 10,000 pieces of chewing gum.
- 65% of bubble gum is sugar.
- Turkey is home to the most gum companies in the world.
- The biggest bubble gum bubble blown (say that 10 times fast, now!) was 23 inches in diameter.
- chewing gum uses eight facial muscles.

Poem about chewing gum:

Chew, chew, chewing gum.

Been at it for hours, and my jaw is numb.

Chew, chew, chewing away,

the flavour evaporated yesterday.

Chew, chew, chew, chew,

chewing gum is such a ruse.

You don't get to eat it, you throw it away,

with a flavour best described as "okay".

But oh, how boring my day would be,

without my chewing gum to accompany me.

8
SOAP

If you don't use this every day, use it every day.

To understand the history of soap, you first have to understand what soap is. Soap is essentially a long fatty acid chain (big molecule) reacting with an alkali. The fatty acid is usually from vegetable oils or animal fats, and the alkali would be a form of lye, coming in the form usually of potassium hydroxide or sodium hydroxide. That's it. And water, but everything has water. The process of making soap is called *saponification*. Big word, simple process.

This big word originates from the Romans, coming from the word *sapo*, meaning "soap" in Latin. It first appears in a book written by Pliny the Elder (great name), where he uses it as a pomade for his hair in the first century BC. It is legend that this soap was produced on Sapo Hill, and was the place where women would wash their clothes in a tributary of the river Tiber. This was a tributary with clay banks, and was below the site of an animal sacrifice site. The women notices that the clothes became clean when it touched and was washed with the soapy clay; this clay was formed from the animal fat from the animal sacrifices being soaked into wood ashes, which then went into the soil. From here: soap.

Mentioned previously in this book as well, the Romans used urine to wash their clothes, which worked well as it contained ammonia. When washing, it formed ammonia carbonate, which reacted with the oils and fats in the woollen clothing to make soap, cleaning the clothes. When in Rome, wash your clothes with urine.

This wasn't the first time soap was used, however. The ancient Babylonians boiled fat, specifically cassia oil, with ashes and water to create the first soap in 2800 BC; the formula for this was written on a clay tablet in order for the soap to be replicated and produced for selling in large quantities.

It was more than just the Babylonians though, with the Egyptians putting their foot in the door as well, bathing in animal and vegetable oils with alkaline salts and creating soap. This was mentioned on the Ebers Papyrus, which also stated it was used to treat sores and skin diseases. Not bad for no internet.

However, this isn't the bar soap that we all know today. It took until the 8th century AD when, in the Islamic Middle East, modern soap was made using olive oil (what's used mostly today) and lime. Made in Syria, it was exported to other parts of the Muslim world, making its way to Europe as well. Soap became a huge part of the economy in the Middle East and soap manufacturing sources cropped up in Damascus, Aleppo, Fes and Nabulus.

There was still soap production as a hangover from the Roman Empire, with Medieval Spain being a leading front in soapmaking in 800, closely followed by the English. Soap-making was a rather progressive profession as well and it was stated that both "women's work and good workmen" were necessary to make high-quality soap. Unfortunately, the soap smelled dreadful (go figure, it was unscented animal fats) and was extremely hard, meaning it was nowhere near as popular as it is today. It took the spices being imported from the Middle East for soap to smell nice, but this only happened in the 15th century. The soap industry boomed after this, with Marseille, France, becoming the leaders and the English working away in London to race to supply the world with soap. How exciting.

It took until the 18th century for soaps to be put to proper use as they'd only just discovered the link between cleanliness and health, mainly in Europe and America. This was big news coming into the Industrial Revolution when soaps could now be mass produced all across America and Europe. This allowed for commercialisation, with many people hopping on the bandwagon for soap making, including William Hesketh Lever and James Lever, two brothers who were making small hand-made soaps before the Industrial Revolution. William Lever was a MP for the Liberal Party and was a huge advocate for expanding the British Empire in the 19th and 20th century, specifically advancing the borders into Africa and Asia where palm oil was imported. This was for his own benefit, as he'd then be able to mass produce soap for a cheaper price. Successful in his ventures, he had wealth, and put a lot of it into marketing and advertisement. This paid off massively for the brothers and they became a household name all across the world known as Unilever: a company that now has an annual turnover of over EUR 50 billion.

It was around the late 1800s where B.J. Johnson developed the first liquid soap, as well as "Palmolive" soap, which quickly became a huge name in the soap industry.

Keep That Wedding Day Complexion

The blushing bride of today should be the blooming matron of tomorrow, retaining the charm of girlhood's freshness to enhance radiant maturity.

For bridal beauty should not fade, nor the passing of each anniversary be recorded on your face.

Keep the schoolgirl complexion which graced your wedding day, and you will keep your youth. With a fresh, smooth skin, no woman ever seems old.

The problem of keeping such a complexion was solved centuries ago. The method is simple—the means within the reach of all.

Cosmetic cleansing the secret

To keep your complexion fresh and smooth you must keep it scrupulously clean. You can't allow dirt, oil and perspiration to collect and clog the pores if you value clearness and fine texture.

You can't depend on cold cream to do this cleansing—repeated applications help fill up the pores. The best way is to wash your face with the mild, soothing lather blended from palm and olive oils, the cleanser used by Cleopatra.

Science has combined those two Oriental oils in the bland, balmy facial soap which bears their name. You need never be afraid of the effects of soap and water if the soap you use is Palmolive.

How it acts

The rich, profuse lather, massaged into the skin, penetrate the pores and removes every trace of the clogging accumulations which, when neglected, make the skin texture coarse and cause blackheads and blotches.

It softens the skin and keeps it flexible and smooth. It freshens and stimulates, encouraging firmness and attractive natural color.

Oily skins won't need cold creams or lotions after using Palmolive. If the skin is inclined to dryness, the time to apply cold cream is after this cosmetic cleansing.

And remember, powder and rouge are perfectly harmless when applied to a clean skin and removed carefully once a day.

Don't keep it only for your face

Complexion beauty should extend to the throat, neck and shoulders. These are quite as conspicuous as your face for beauty or the lack of it.

Give them the same beautifying cleansing that you do your face and they will become soft, white and smooth. Use it regularly for bathing and let it do for your body what it does for your face.

Not too expensive

Although Palmolive is the finest, mildest facial soap that can be produced, the price is not too high to permit general use in the washstand for bathing.

This enormous price is due to popularity, to the enormous demand which keeps the Palmolive factories working day and night, and necessitates the importation of the costly oils in vast quantity.

Thus, soap which would cost at least 25 cents a cake if made in small quantities, is offered for only 10 cents, a price all can afford. The old-time luxury of the few may now be enjoyed the world over.

THE PALMOLIVE COMPANY, Milwaukee, U.S.A.
THE PALMOLIVE COMPANY OF CANADA, Limited, Toronto, Ontario

Volume and efficiency
produce 25-cent quality
for
10c

Advertisement for Palmolive in 1922

Making soaps now is a semi-mainstream hobby as it's easy to do. Most of the soap-making process occurs in a kettle and, by the end of it, you'll have a very clean kettle and some gross tasting tea.

Other facts that didn't make the cut:

- One million deaths could be prevented each year if people washed their hands with soap.
- Soap carving is 10/10 on my satisfying scale. Look it up.
- Www.soaphistory.net lists 14 types of soap. Try and name five. I dare you.
- There aren't that many facts about soap that haven't been mentioned already.
- Peasants in Russia used lye instead of soap, which causes vomiting, diarrhoea and even death.
- The world's most expensive soap costs $2,800 per bar. It's infused with diamond and gold powder. Why tho?
- William Lever bought a painting called *Bubbles*. Coincidence? I think not.
- William Lever also used tactics of forced labour in order for his soap to be made.
- Lever's forced labour was compared to the Holocaust by Belgian authorities.
- Unilever was the world's first multinational company.
- By 1930, Unilever employed over 250,000 people, making it the largest company in Britain at the time.
- Children under the age of five reduce their risk of pneumonia by 50% if they wash their hands with soap.
- Soap operas are called so as they were first sponsored and produced by Proctor and Gamble, a major soap company in the 1930s and even today.

Poem about soap:

Soapy bubbles make me clean,

and make my life more evergreen.

If you don't use it, then you're gross,

being the person in the room that smells the most.

Your face, your back, your pits, your knees,

use it everywhere as you please.

Please use soap, I beg of you.

If you don't, you'll smell like a zoo.

9
FIZZY DRINKS

No one really knows what to call fizzy drinks. Wikipedia has a whole page dedicated to the name of "soft drinks" in the United States. I've decided to keep you on your toes and switch up what I call it until I run out of words to use.

As with many tasty things, pop may have originated in the medieval Middle East when fruits were infused into drinks, such as *sherbat*: a drink made with cane juice. This drink is where we get the English word "sherbet" from. Syrups and honey were also used alongside mint and "jujube", which might be my new favourite word. Flavoured drinks spread like wildfire around Europe, with the *Water Imperial* being invented in Tudor England (16th century) soon after: an early lemonade flavoured with lemon and sweetened with cream of tartar.

However, none of these drinks were fizzy, and therefore, we cannot call them soda, but they were an early precursor. To understand the history of soda, we have to take into the consideration of fizziness and what it is.

The fizz in a drink is just dissolved carbon dioxide, put there under immense pressures. When the pressure is released, so is the carbon dioxide, coming out in the form of small bubbles. That's it.

It took until 1767, when Johnathon Priestly was playing around with gases, for carbonated water to be invented. Priestly, in my eyes, must be one of the smartest people to have ever lived. He has over 100 works that he invented, including work that revolutionised grammar, religion, politics and, most notably, science. He's credited with the discovery of oxygen, carbon monoxide, nitric oxide, nitrous oxide, ammonia, sulphur dioxide, nitrogen peroxide, the carbon cycle *and* carbonated water. This man fit all of this in his life, all while almost being killed by his own country as he was a Dissenter (a person who did not conform with the Church of England). People of his own town of Birmingham even burned down his house. Yes, I have a bit of a man crush on Priestly.

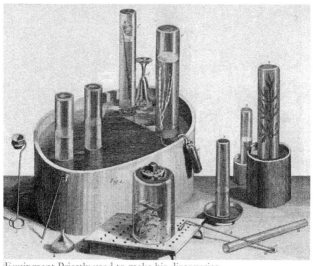

Equipment Priestly used to make his discoveries.

Anyway, back to fizzy pop.

The way Priestly did it was by suspending a bowl of distilled water above a beer vat in Leeds, which was the start of soft drinks. Soon after, Priestly published a paper called "Impregnating Water with Fixed Air". Bit weird but okay.

After this, people tried and tried to commercialise it, mostly for medicinal purposes. But it took Johann Joseph Schweppe in 1783 to develop mass-produced carbonated water. Sound familiar? With the success of the soft drink, Schweppe founded the company that we know to be Schweppes today. This company became such a success that it even received a royal warrant from King William IV as he liked his carbonated water so much.

This takes us to the 1840s when soda pop was a booming industry with over 50 manufacturers all around the world. Lemonade was the big seller and Schweppes as the big name in the industry. There was just one big problem: how do you store carbonated water?

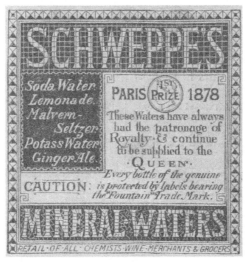

Advertisement for Schweppes in 1878.

Sealing the bottles was a big issue, especially as they'd be under immense pressure from the carbonation. This was until Hiram Codd patented the Codd-neck bottle. I'd put a picture in, but it's honestly so phallic it might as well be pornography. When the automatic glass blowing machine received a patent, glass bottle production increased by 50 times, meaning soda was more available than ever. It was around this time (late 19th century) that the familiar name of Coca-Cola Company was founded. It was founded by pharmacist John Stith Pemberton in Columbus, Georgia, and was invented for headache relief... kind of. Pemberton was a Confederate Colonel who was wounded in the American Civil War and was addicted to morphine. In a desperate attempt to wean himself off, he created *Pemberton's French Wine Coca* as a nerve tonic. This couldn't have been much better than the morphine, as Pemberton called for caffeine and cocaine as the main two ingredients. Yikes.

Pemberton patented his "drink" as medicine, saying it could cure morphine addiction, indigestion, nerve disorders, headaches and impotence. Cola became a hit, initially selling at five-cents a glass and is now the biggest name in soft drinks. At its peak, Coca-Cola employed over 100,000 members of staff.

Today, an unholy number of soft drinks are drunk every day, with the annual average consumption in the USA at 153 litres — twice that of the UK — despite everyone knowing the risks involved (which include obesity, dental decay, kidney stones, and even cancer). I'm even writing this while drinking some.

Woops.

Other facts that didn't make the cut:

- The original name for 7-Up was *Bib-Label Lithiated Lemon-Lime Soda*. Catchy.
- Acid levels of soda and batteries are the same.
- Coca-Cola uses 17.4% of all aluminium in the USA each year.
- One can of fizzy drink allegedly speeds up the ageing process by 4.6 years.
- When the Pepsi slogan "Come alive with Pepsi!" was translated into Chinese, it read "Pepsi brings back your ancestors back from the grave!". Great marketing.
- Americans consume over 1.7 million tons of sugar from fizzy drinks each year.
- You can use soda to remove stains from a toilet bowl. Not surprised this one didn't make it in.
- Studies show that men prefer drinks that don't contain the word *diet* as well as darker drinks.
- You can get a black garlic flavoured soda in Switzerland.
- A can of Coke contains about half the amount of caffeine than the same amount of coffee.
- Coke contains high levels of 4-methylimidazole, a known carcinogen.
- In 1916, the American Government tried to get Coca-Cola to remove caffeine from its drinks.
- There are many discontinued flavours of Coke, including green tea, raspberry and bacon.

Poem about fizzy drinks:

Fizzy pop, fizzy drinks.

some are brown, some are pink.

Drink too many and you'll find

that it's hard to unwind.

Lots of sugar, here and there,

substantially more than a prickly pear.

Try to limit to one a day.

The rest? Throw them away.

Fizzy pop, fizzy drinks.

Call them what you like,

Before you have one, have a think,

on the affect it has on your life.

10
VEGETARIANISM

Adolf Hitler, Forest Whitaker, Nikola Tesla. The thing that links them? They're vegetarians. You may ask: "Why not write about vegans?". Well, I don't know if I could bring myself to research and write about veganism for hours and hours. So, here we are. Vegetarianism.

It's possible that vegetarianism started around the 6th century BC. This was in the Indian subcontinent where Buddhism and Jainism were popular. Both promoted vegetarianism, but Jain was stricter. Parshva, the earliest Jain leader, preached nonviolence and it became one of the "Five Yamas", or five vows that Jainism was founded upon. As Jainism and Buddhism grew in the Indian subcontinent, vegetarianism became enshrined in their history and carries forward into today's culture. One Chinese pilgrim named Faxian travelled to India circa the 5th century CE, stating

"India is a strange country. People do not kill any living creatures, do not keep pigs and fowl, and do not sell live cattle."

Vegetarianism is also essential in many Hindus' way of life, and killing a cow in Hinduism is a sin. No steak for you.

This takes us onto the Ancient Greeks, surprise surprise. During the classical antiquity (big words for between the 8th century BC and 6th century AD), the Greeks named the vegetarian diet "abstinence begins with the soul", which I think would be a less popular name nowadays. The group of people that ate vegetarian food was small, but they were loyal. Pythagoras was a loyal one of those followers and was described by Plato as "distinguished by such purity and so avoided killing and killers that he not only abstained from animal foods, but even kept his distance from cooks and hunters.". Not only this, but Pythagoras made GCSE maths a pain in the ass.

Pythagoras

Almost all Stoic scholars in the classical antiquity were very anti-vegetarianism, as they insisted on the absence of reason in brutes, which led them to conclude that there can't be any ethical obligations or restraints in dealing with the world of animals. Seems a bit drawn out to me.

The Middle Ages were also a big time for the vegetarians, with the Rule of St Benedict being enforced. This rule said that monks were able to eat fish and fowl, but nothing that had four legs unless the monk was ill. Even then, they knew that having a burger would make you feel better. Although this was a big time for vegetarianism, it was also a big time for anti-vegetarianism, with theologians such as St Augustine and St Thomas Aquinas saying that "man owes no duties to animals" — a huge blow for the vegetarians. 0-1 to the anti-veggies.

Along comes Leonardo da Vinci: a man known for his inventions and paintings and fantastic beard. He read up about Pythagoras and adopted a Pythagorean way of life, influencing philosophers and writers such as Descartes and many other Romantic poets. 1-1.

By the 18th century, people were prepping for the arrival in America. One of those people was Benjamin Franklin. The inventor, mathematician, Founding Father among more, was also a vegetarian. Almost, anyway. When he was a teenager, he was an apprentice in a print shop, and came across a book advocating vegetarianism by Thomas Tyron. This would've been in line with the morals put forward by the Pennsylvanian Quakers (who were vegetarian) that he was surrounded by. He even called the consumption of meat "unprovoked murder", although is said to have been tempted by fried cod of all things. Tut tut. On vegetarianism, Franklin said:

"When about 16 years of age, I happen'd to meet with a book written by one Tryon, recommending a vegetable diet. I determined to go into it ... [By not eating meat] I presently found that I could save half what [my brother] paid me. This was an additional fund for buying books: but I had another advantage in it ... I made the greater progress from that greater clearness of head and quicker apprehension which usually attend temperance in eating and drinking."

It's also true that Franklin suffered from obesity, but hey ho.

By the 19th century, vegetarianism was associated with cultural reform movements, such as those that advocated temperance and were avidly against vivisection, with vegetarianism being propagated as an essential part of "the natural way of life". In 1812, the first vegetarian cookbook was published with the catchy name: *"Vegetable Cookery: With an Introduction, Recommending Abstinence from Animal Food and Intoxicating Liquors".* Another one that rolls off the tongue. Written by Martha Brotherton, published anonymously by a "member of the Bible Christian Church" (who doesn't love a mystery). The book is also said to involve "copious amounts of butter". 2-0 to obesity.

The Vegetarian Society was founded soon after, having 889 members in 1853 and growing to over 4,000 by the end of the century. The members of the Vegetarian Society believed in a simple life and "pure food", whatever that is.

However, in the mid-19th century, many didn't choose the vegetarian lifestyle, the vegetarian lifestyle chose them. Many adopted vegetarianism because, pound for pound, meat was far more expensive than vegetables. It made more sense for the working class to own living meat than for them to kill it and eat it.

This was the time of Leo Tolstoy who was an avid supporter of vegetarianism in Russia. Mid-20th century, Hitler came along and adopted a vegetarian diet in the 1930s. It's said that at social events, he gave graphic accounts of animals being slaughtered to sway them off meat. This, from the man that killed millions of people. Hitler was actually surprisingly healthy. He quit smoking and alcohol and became a vegetarian. That was until he started using amphetamines.

Honestly, there's not much more to vegetarianism than that. How much more could being vegetarian change? All it is, is not eating meat.

Other facts that didn't make the cut:

- Indian vegetarians make up about 70% of the vegetarians in the world.
- There are two legally vegetarian towns in India.
- 14% of the UK population are vegetarian.
- There's such thing as a *fruitarian*, someone who eats fruits, nuts and seeds without killing the plant.
- Plants provide 10 times more protein per acre than meat.
- A British study claims that children with a higher IQ are more likely to become vegetarian.
- One pound of wheat requires 25 gallons of water for production. One pound of meat requires 2,500 gallons.
- Other famous vegetarians include: Benedict Cumberbatch, Natalie Portman, Bill Clinton, Zac Efron and Madonna.
- Vegans and vegetarians are at a higher risk of depression due to decreased omega-3 consumption.
- The word *vegan* is derived from the word *vegetarian*. The creator just used the first letters of the word *vegetarian*.
- If a man stops eating red meat, it increases the "sex appeal" of his odour. Musky.
- The average American eats 222 pounds of meat a year, not including seafood.
- In 2012, the Los Angeles city council unanimously decided that every Monday, it'll be meatless.

Poem about vegetarianism:

Don't eat meat. Don't do it. It's bad.

Especially when you see your dad,

who scoffs down chicken wings like never before,

and orders steaks in amounts galore.

Have some lentils, have some fruit.

Maybe then, you'll fit in your suit.

But don't use copious amounts of butter,

Like Martha and Ben, 'cus you'll get fatter.

Veggies are good. Veggies are great!

Veggies make you eat all on your plate.

You'll save the animals, maybe yourself.

Add the veggie cookbook to your shelf.

Give it a go. Give it a try.

What's the worst that can happen! You're not going to die.

11
CHOCOLATE

Writing this gave me more cravings than the donut chapter.

Chocolate must be one of the greatest foodstuffs that was ever invented. Chocolate and coffee is an unbeatable combination, but chocolate by itself is also fantastic. If I get through writing this without ordering a bunch of chocolate online, then I deserve a medal. If you read this and do the same, you deserve one, too.

Chocolate may date back to 1750 BC or earlier, with the Mesoamericans being the first to take advantage of the cocoa bean. Native to the area, the beans weren't in short supply and were cultivated to produce 30 to 40 reddish-brown almond shaped beans per sheath of a cocoa tree. These beans are bitter, but have a sweet, addictive pulp exploited by humans. There's evidence of a chocolate martini of sorts, fermented and served as an alcoholic drink. Why isn't this common today?

This drink was used as an offering to the gods, and its scientific name is *Theobroma cacao*, meaning "food of the gods".

The Mayans and the Aztecs used the bean for everything, believing it had divine properties. It was used in rituals of birth, marriage, and death. Human sacrifices were given chocolate to cheer up before the deed was done. This would cheer me up to be fair. The blood of the sacrifice would then be drunk, mixed with a cocoa-derived drink. Bleurgh.

The Mayans also used to season their chocolate, usually with chilli peppers and cornmeal. Cocoa beans were also used as currency A rabbit was worth around 10 cocoa beans and the services of a prostitute being worth around the same amount, but "according to how they agree", it was subject to change.

The Aztecs had it slightly more difficult as they were unable to grow the cocoa trees in their soil, meaning it had to be imported. This meant it was slightly more expensive, but it was equally if not more important than cocoa in the Mayan empire. The Aztecs believed that one of their gods, Quetzalcoatl, God of Wind and Wisdom, was a feathered serpent that created the boundary between the earth and the sky and was cast away by the other gods for sharing chocolate with mankind. The other gods didn't feel like the people were deserving of something so delicious, so they cast him away after he stole the cocoa tree from his brother's back garden. This meant the Aztecs felt blessed to have such a divine bean as it was from the gods. It was consumed as "cold-chocolate", usually as an aphrodisiac or as a post-banquet treat.

Enter: the Spaniards.

1502 comes around and Christopher Columbus is on his fourth trip to the Americas. He comes across the cocoa tree and, upon seeing the importance of the beans to the Aztecs, he seized a great number of the trees and took them back with him to Spain. Unknown to most, Columbus was really a dreadful human being. He's credited with being the first one to know that the world was round, but this was common knowledge when he set sail. Not only that, but he killed thousands of indigenous people and kept many women imprisoned for months to rape them. He forced the indigenous into labour to find gold. If they didn't fill their quota, he cut off their hands and let them bleed to death. Not really craving chocolate anymore.

Columbus' son, Ferdinand, said the following about the beans:

"for when they were brought on board ship together with their goods, I observed that when any of these almonds fell, they all stooped to pick it up, as if an eye had fallen."

Nothing really happened with the beans until the time of Montezuma, ninth ruler of the Aztec Empire. In the courts, Montezuma had a constant supply of the cocoa drink, as it (supposedly) brought him power over women. The Spanish saw this, and saw the women serve Montezuma soon after. They were in awe. How could such a drink have so much power?

They were quick to import it back to Spain where chocolate was first used as a medicine after they observed the Aztecs drink it to reduce inflammation, but they were fast to make it tasty. They sweetened it with honey to counteract the natural bitterness and got rid of the spices that the Aztecs put in. This new chocolate swept across Europe — and swept fast. From the 17th to 19th century, there was a so-called "chocolate craze". As many of the natives of South America had died from the STIs and diseases brought over by the Spanish, they turned to African slaves as their labourers who, unfortunately, bore the brunt of this chocolate craze. In 1729, the first mechanical cocoa grinder was invented in Bristol, UK, with the sole purpose of "expeditious, fine and clean making of chocolate by engine". This pre-industrial revolution machine made it easier for chocolate to go mainstream, but it wasn't quite there yet. It was the Dutch in 1815 that did this, with the chemist Coenraad van Houten being the first to add alkaline salts to chocolate to take away its bitterness. He created the press to remove the cacao butter, again, making it cheaper and easier to make. John Cadbury (the name is a big hint) visited van Houten and saw the press, thought it was fantastic, and started selling chocolate in 1875, the same year milk chocolate was invented by Daniel Peter, whose neighbour was none other than Henri Nestlé. It seems that chocolate's success is one big coincidence. Rudolf Lindt invented the first conching machine to make chocolate smooth and shiny, Nestlé and Cadbury had set up their own companies and Milton S. Hershey bought and set up equipment to make chocolate-covered caramels. The chocolate industry was booming.

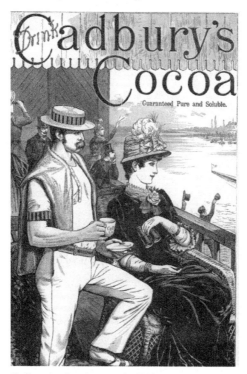

Cadbury's advertisement in 1885.

This was until the 20th century when people started becoming *woke*. Cadbury, amongst others, was caught in scandal for their use of West African slave plantations and often using children. This is still a problem today with only 5% of the world's chocolate being produce in line with the regulations set out by Fairtrade in 2008. We all like to think we are *woke*, so next time you buy chocolate, make sure it has the Fairtrade mark on it before you walk up to the till.

Other facts that didn't make the cut:

- Chocolate has been sent on every American space mission.
- On average, a person eats 5kg of chocolate a year. The Swiss average is 10kg.
- American chocolate companies use 680,000,000kg of milk a year.
- Over 17,000 people in Belgium work in the chocolate industry.
- Scientists are creating climate-change-resistant chocolate through DNA editing.
- the biggest chocolate bar ever made weighed 5,800kg. That's over five Honda Civics.
- You have to eat 10kg of chocolate before it becomes toxic.
- Dark chocolate has a high caffeine content.
- Milton S. Hershey was due to go on the Titanic but cancelled his trip last minute.
- The FDA allows 60 pieces of insect per 100 grams of chocolate produced, as well as one rodent hair and even rodent faeces.
- The second mention of Alfred Hitchcock's *Psycho* in this book: Hitchcock used chocolate syrup as blood in the famous shower scene.
- Hershey's produces 70 million chocolate kisses each *day*.
- Only dark chocolate is beneficial to human health and it's only the case when cacao is the first ingredient listed, not sugar.
- In WWII, the Germans designed a chocolate bar that detonated seven seconds after a piece of it was broken off.

Poem about chocolate:

The chocolate melts,

I undo my belt,

to fit it into my belly.

I have to admit,

I'm quite unfit

and full of chocolate and jelly.

But I can't stop,

I go to the shop,

buy it, and sit by the TV.

Eaten in a flash

after bangers and mash

watching a season three.

The chocolate is gone,

I've had my fun,

and I'll have to buy some more.

Until tomorrow,

There'll be no sorrow.

Chocolate? It'll not bore.

THE HISTORY OF SOME STUFF

12
BRAS

Why bras? Honestly, don't know.

Bras have *kind of* been around for centuries. I say kind of because the first bras weren't really bras, they were sort of opposite bras. They were a type of fitted corset that had no area covering the breast. Hence, me saying, "opposite bra". The first instance of this was the Minoan Snake Goddess, Faience, way back in ancient Crete circa 1600 BC. This wasn't the only instance of bras in ancient Greece, with Book 14 of Homer's *Iliad* referring to the "embroidered girdle" of Aphrodite, which is what I think all bras should be called actually. Goddesses were commonly seen with a strap around the breast, called a *stróphion*, translated as a twisted band. Although we don't know whether wearing one of these was an everyday thing, we do see evidence from statues and other artworks that they did exist, commonplace or not. We also know that bandeau-like strips of cloth were worn around the breasts of athletic women when participating in sport; the first sports bra.

A mosaic depicting women playing sport wearing a very, very early version of a sports bra.

Indecency was a word being used more and more coming into the Middle Ages, and bras weren't that common. There is some evidence to suggest they were around, most notably by Henri de Mondeville, surgeon to King Phillip the Fair of France (great name), who wrote of "breastbags", which might've been worn to flatten the breast if needed. Yet, the lack of evidence suggests bras still weren't all that common.

From the 16th century onwards, corsets were the bee's knees (dog's bollocks, cat's meow, fox's socks, etc.), and bras were left in the dust. It took another three centuries for bras to become more normal. People were only wearing corsets if they were very wealthy, and only at social events due to the health problems caused by them. A prominent figure for getting bras into the market and making them normal was Amelia Bloomer. Bloomer was the first woman to own, edit and publish a newspaper, which she called *The Lily*. With this platform, Bloomer was able to speak her mind, something that wasn't normal in society. Bloomer could talk about women wearing pants, as well as letting other women know what was *in*, including "bloomers", named after Bloomer.

It was a man by the name of Henry S. Lesher who patented a device to give "symmetrical rotundity" to the wearer's breast in 1859 and a similar device was patented by Luman L. Chapman three years later that he called a "corset substitute". Historians commonly refer to this as the *proto-bra*.

Hermaine Cadolle invented the first modern bra, calling it "the well-being" and using elastic and straps to support breasts via the shoulders, but it's not quite the bra we all know today.

In 1910, Mary Phelps Jacob was a 19-year-old socialite in New York City, wanting to wear a beautiful gown she had chosen for a ball. However, the gown had a plunging neckline and wasn't suitable for her as she had rather large breasts. The only acceptable undergarment at that time was a corset. But the whole outfit just didn't work. She called up her maid who made a bra to suit her outfit out of two handkerchiefs and some pink ribbon. She was a hit at the ball, with people offering her money for her work. She went on to patent her invention, which she sold for $1,500 or over $22,000 in modern-day money.

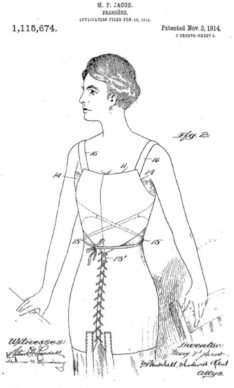

Jacob's patent for a bra.

The 1920s came along, and along with it came the Flappers. These were women that expressed "boyish" characteristics and flouted the societal restrictions on what being a woman meant. To achieve the Flapper silhouette, women wore bras to decrease their breast size, creating a more androgenous figure. Bras became commonplace, but it was the 30s when bras were really revolutionised. The word *bra* was starting to be used in everyday conversation as a shortened version of brasserie. The first bras with sizing became available in sizes A through D. Before this, the sizes were nicknamed egg cup, teacup, coffee cup and challenge cup. Two major companies set the standard for all other bras when they started using letters for sizing. It was all about the silhouette, with a lot of women wanting a "pointy bust". This, with clever advertisement exploiting the Hollywood glamour, bra sales went through the roof. In the 50s, the term "sweater girl" was coined, aided by the likes of the *bullet bra",* making breasts stand out when wearing a sweater. Seeing Hollywood celebrities such as Patti Page and Marilyn Monroe wear such bras made them desirable, and people were loving them. The use of television for advertisement was used in the 80s as well, with many actresses wearing the likes of a Wonderbra on TV. Unfortunately, many of these actresses were forced to wear such bras to emphasize their breasts and had to undo a button or two with the hopes of increasing viewership.

Undoubtedly, there have been multiple shifts in the timeline of bras concerning whether they should be for fashion or whether they should be for comfort. In 2017, Marks & Spencer saw a 45% decrease in cleavage-boosting bras, and a 40% increase in wireless bras (for all the men out there that don't know anything, these aren't bras you can connect to your phone via Bluetooth, they just don't contain any wires). Bras definitely have their place in history and have a strong link with early feminism, but it seems that they're on the decline. But this decline still has this link with feminism as the no-bra movement becomes more and more popular.

It's unfortunate that even today, women don't have the same privileges that men do. Can bras change that? I don't know, but they can certainly play their part.

Other facts that didn't make the cut:

- According to fashionista.com, 85% of women are wearing the wrong bra size.
- There's a myth that underwired bras cause breast cancer. This is obviously not true.
- Neil Armstrong's space suit was made by Playtex, a bra manufacturer.
- The largest bra ever was over 375 square meters and weighed 95kg.
- Victoria's Secret created a bra worth $15 million.
- The average breast weighs one pound.
- During WWII, a bra was invented that turned into two gas masks.
- Mark Twain invented and patented the bra clasp.
- There was a $500 fine if a Playboy Bunny took a suit home.
- To hit the high note in Goldfinger, Shirley Bassey had to remove her bra in between takes in the studio.
- Ke$ha used teeth from her fans to create a bra. Umm…
- There's a Japanese bra that analyses your heart rate amongst other things to determine whether you are "in love". If you are, then the bra automatically unhooks. Saucy.
- There's a bra connected to Twitter, which tweets every time it's unhooked, reminding people to self-check themselves for lumps and bumps.

Acrostic poem about bras:

Buy the

Right size.

Apt poem for chapter about bras.

13
BISCUITS

Being British, I love a cup of tea. This means I also love a good dunk of a biscuit into tea. I'd write about the history of tea but it's just not fun, and it's very complicated. So, to save myself a headache, here's the history of the biscuit.

It's unfortunate that the first biscuits were so disgusting and not coated in milk chocolate, although that would've made for a very short chapter. The first biscuits were what are now known as hardtack. The Romans and Egyptians had similar versions but not much is known about them, although they served the same purpose: biscuits were an easy source of calories, and therefore, sustenance. They didn't spoil easily and could be kept around, literally, for years. The Romans spread boiled flour on a plate, waited for it to harden, cut, fried and served with honey and pepper. Doesn't even sound that bad.

Hardtack is thought to have first been mass produced by the Royal Navy in the 1660s, with sailors having one biscuit and a gallon of beer a day. Sounds alright to me. To make sure the biscuits didn't spoil, every last bit of moisture had to be expelled during the cooking process. This meant these biscuits were cooked over and over and over again. Imagine a rock being put in an oven. That's what this is. Although they were hard, it meant they had a shelf-life of years and years. In the US Civil War, troops were given biscuits as rations that were prepared for the Mexican-American War, 15 years prior.

To eat these, sailors would have to boil them in anything they could get their hands on, whether that be coffee, beer, water, anything. As you can imagine, eating them day after day became boring, so various "recipes" have been made using the hardtack by the sailors. The biscuits were crushed and boiled into a porridge to get the calories needed and a fire was used to blacken the biscuit, crush it and infuse it in water to create a make-shift coffee, or fry it in a pan.

Putting the biscuit in water had more than one function, however. Ships in the 17th and 18th century didn't exactly scream cleanliness, meaning parasites and worms were everywhere. When put into water, the worms and other bugs would be drawn out, giving rise to the name "worm castles", a common name for hardtack among sailors. Of course, all the bugs were to the sailors was protein, so many just chomped away without a worry in the world.

Next along came *water biscuits* in 1801, when Josiah Bent started selling them at the port of Boston, as they also didn't deteriorate. Water biscuits were a great food source for the poor that flocked to the California mines, sold in wagon trains. Bent, with his newfound small fortune, founded the G. H. Bent Company, which produced hardtack in the American Civil War, and still makes the same hardtack to this day, usually sold to those who re-enact the Civil War.

Speaking of the American Civil War, biscuits were unbelievably important. They were the main food source for many soldiers, although they weren't very popular. Soldiers sang a song titled *Hard Tack Come Again No More*, sung to the tune of *Hard Times Come Again No More*, describing the biscuits as "old and very wormy". Yummy.

Hardtack remained standard until canned food rations were implemented in 1847, but some hardtack still existed. There's hardtack from this era that can still be seen today in museums, such as the Maritime Museum in Kronborg, Denmark, where you can find hardtack from 1852. And no, there's no mould.

Actual yummy biscuits have been around for even longer than hardtack but weren't popular. It's possible that in the 7th century, there were cooks in the Persian empire who sweetened bread-based mixtures with honey and fruit. It's more of a fruit-bread than a biscuit, but hey, I've written about it anyway.

Another example of this is gingerbread, which was made as early as the 10th century by Armenian monk Grégoire de Nicopolis, which he called *"pain d'épices"*, or *spice bread*. But again, more of a bread than a biscuit. Greg, as I'll now call him because his name is hard to spell, lived in France after he left Lesser Armenia, and the locals loved him. He taught the Christians and the priests how to cook gingerbread but it was so expensive to make due to the treacle and molasses. So, the cooks felt like they needed to use every last bit of the mixture. The leftovers were used to make the first ever ginger biscuits. Finally, a nice biscuit.

Gingerbread biscuits in 1605 started to look like the gingerbread men that we eat today, and it's all thanks to Guy Fawkes. After he was foiled and unsuccessfully blew up Parliament, people made gingerbread biscuits in the shape of his body and ate it, showing their support to Parliament by eating the villain. Yea, that'll show 'em.

The industry of tasty biscuits didn't really go anywhere until the Industrial Revolution, when biscuits were mass produced for a cheaper price. One of those biscuits is a name that we all know and love, the Digestive. Despite it being a good dunk in a cup of tea, they weren't marketed as a sweet treat. Originating in Scotland, two doctors developed the Digestive to aid digestion. This was because of the sodium bicarbonate added to the biscuit, used to "digest" starch. They were first advertised in 1876, and have grown to be one of the most popular biscuits ever. 80 million packs are sold annually, with chocolate Digestives being called a "British masterpiece" by Bill Bryson. I couldn't agree more.

I decided not to cover this chapter in pictures, because a biscuit is a biscuit. They all look pretty similar. Instead of pictures though, I'll give you a recipe for hardtack, as I've described it as a coveted meal and so delicious:

Ingredients:
- 4 ½ cups of flour
- 2 cups of water
- 3 teaspoons of salt
- more than half a brain cell

Method

1. Mix all the ingredients together until it makes a fairly dry dough.
2. Roll the dough so that it is about ½ inch thick.
3. Cut into squares with the size of your liking.
4. Poke a few holes using a toothpick so that it looks authentic, and you can pretend to be a sailor.
5. Place on an ungreased baking sheet and cook for 30 minutes at 190°C.
6. You can do what you like with them as they're done now, but it's recommended you let them dry out for a few days, then soak in water or milk for 10-15 minutes and fry in a buttered skillet. Add a little salt, and voila.

Other facts that didn't make the cut:

- There's a teahouse in Brighton that doesn't allow people to dunk their biscuits in tea.
- Chocolate Digestives have chocolate on the bottom, not the top.
- In 2009, a study found that 25 million Brits were injured by biscuits.
- Rich Tea biscuits were developed for the wealthy to enjoy between meals.
- William and Kate had a Rich Tea wedding cake.
- The highest dunk in the world was from a 230ft bungee jump. Simon Berry jumped off the platform holding a Chocolate Hobnob and dunked it into a cup of tea at the bottom.
- Australian biscuit company Arnott's holds the world's largest collection of baby photos.
- National Biscuit Day is held on the 29th of May each year.
- If you were to line up every Jaffa Cake eaten a year, it would stretch from the UK to Australia.
- 61% of the UK own a biscuit tin.
- It takes seven minutes to bake a Digestive.
- Sadiq Khan's favourite biscuit is the Chocolate Hobnob.
- Boris Johnson used Mumsnet to announce his favourite biscuit. I won't say what his choice was as I don't was to ruin the biscuit.
- Rich Tea biscuits can withstand 14 dunks, according to the McVitie's food scientist.
- According to the same scientist, you should leave your tea for three minutes before dunking.

THE HISTORY OF SOME STUFF

Sea shanty about biscuits (make up your own tune if you like):

Ill sing ye a song, a song of the sea,

'nd you dip yer biscuit in that tea.

I'm stuck on the ship, drinking my grog,

You have yer tea in a flask, walking yer dog.

Yo ho ho, I'm eating hardtack,

But we're runnin' out, not many in the stack.

Aye aye, I take a swig of my rum.

Sitting down 'urts, there's a boil on me bum.

Four cups of flour and a sprinkle of salt,

dipped in my beer made from malt.

It doesn't taste nice, it doesn't taste great,

Barely keeps me alive and has bugs that we hate.

Yo ho ho, I'm eating hardtack,

But we're runnin' out, not many in the stack.

Aye aye, I take a swig of my rum.

Sitting down 'urts, there's a boil on me bum.

14

GLASSES

Glasses, are without a doubt, one of the key inventions of the human race. Okay, bold statement, but they are an absolute necessity for many. So many in fact, that 60% of us wear glasses. Those 40% are gods. We're just mere mortals in comparison.

There were a couple of precursors to glasses, a couple of them enhancing sight, mainly for reading. One of these was the reading stone, a hemispherical lens that was placed on top of writing for those that suffered presbyopia (big word for farsightedness). This was written in Ptolemy's *Optics*, circa 2nd century, but it's possible that these reading stones were only put into practice 900 years later, when Alhazen, dubbed "The Father of Modern Optics" wrote his "Book of Optics", circa 1021. Various other glasses were produced but none with corrective properties, such as the Inuit's snow goggles and the sunglasses of 12th century China, made of beautiful smoky quartz.

The first glasses with any corrective properties were invented by a man with the fantastic name of Roger Bacon. He was the first European to describe the production of gunpowder and was regarded a wizard when he was alive in the 1200s. Bacon wrote multiple works about optics and gunpowder, but his knowledge didn't stop there. He wrote of grammar, stating eloquently "Grammar is one and the same in all languages, substantially, though it may vary, accidentally, in each of them." He invented the Georgian calendar, wrote about specie differentiation, theology, philosophy and more. The main thing is that he also wrote about using lenses for optical purposes in 1268.

The first pair of glasses though, weren't made until 22 years after Bacon's proposal in Pisa. The Dominican friar Giordano da Pisa wrote: "It is not yet twenty years since there was found the art of making eyeglasses, which make for good vision… and it is so short a time that this new art, never before extant, was discovered."

Giordano loved these so much, and started telling everyone about them, including his pal Friar Alessandro della Spina of Pisa (also, great name). Giordano was unwilling to share his creation with the rest of the world but Spina wasn't a fan of this and started making his own, bringing him great joy in spiting the man who didn't share. Within 10 years, there was regulation in Venice, governing the sale of glasses, with the 14th century being the century where glasses became common. It's strange seeing portraits of people from the 14th to the 18th century with glasses on, as it looks like a child has drawn them with a biro on a newspaper. Example:

Fernando Niño de Guevara by El Greco circa 1600, wearing glasses that look like a child has drawn over the portrait to make him look funny. All he needs is a moustache.

The invention of glasses seems something quite coveted, with Marco Polo claiming he saw the invention first in China, and Francesco Redi claiming Salvino degli Aemati invented them in the 13th century. None of them true.

Remember famous obese vegetarian Benjamin Franklin? The Founding Father was also the inventor of the bifocals, which he used for himself as he suffered from both long-sightedness and short-sightedness. Glasses didn't change much besides their style (I think scissor glasses are the epitome of sexy – look them up). After the first lenses were designed to correct astigmatisms, the rest is history. Glasses are glasses.

From the 1930s to the 70s, glasses were seen by many as humiliating as they were an easy disability to make fun of. This was until clever advertisement in the 70s, and the demand for fashionable glasses went through the roof. Many people that have used glasses have them embedded in their personal image, such as the admirable Clark Kent who overcame many obstacles despite his endless battle with vision.

Glasses are so simple, yet so complex. This book wouldn't be possible without them. All they need to do now is invent glasses with a GPS tracker and a speaker so you can ask Alexa where they are, and she'll tell you what room they're in.

Other facts that didn't make it in:

- Wearing glasses doesn't create a dependency on them. Don't be silly.
- As well as bifocals, Franklin invented the lighting rod, swim fins, the urinary catheter and a glass harmonica.
- People estimate that Elton John has anywhere between 2,000 and 250,000 pairs of glasses.
- The record for "The Most Actors Wearing Sunglasses in a Movie" is held by *Matrix*.
- Four million pairs of glasses are thrown away in the US each year.
- Elvis Presley's glasses sold for $250,000 on eBay.
- Emperor Nero used emeralds as glasses so he could see further when watching events.
- Pirates used to wear golden earrings to improve their vision. It didn't work, but hey, placebo.
- Smart glasses will be the second most transformative tech over the next 25 years.
- although a commercial failure, Google Glass has been used around the world for many different purposes, including medical procedures, helping children with autism and even lactation consultation.
- Two thirds of contact lens wearers are female.
- Up to 90% of those that wear contact lenses don't follow the proper hygienic method.
- One in 500 people who use contact lenses will go blind due to improper use or accidents.
- The people of Japan have the worst eyesight in the world. One in 20 Japanese men are colour-blind.

Poem about glasses:

Ah, crap I can't see.

With my glasses, I'll be fine.

I really need to go and pee,

I can't see the loo sign.

What am I to do?

Where am I to go?

Is it right in front of me?

I guess I'll never know.

I dig and search in all my pockets,

to try and find the lens,

But all I find: a toy rocket,

and some lids from a couple of pens.

"Squint! Squint!", but alas, I cannot see.

Oh well, this is it.

But now there's a bigger problem,

because now I need a shit.

15
SURGERY

I can already tell this one's going to be good.

Modern day surgery has saved countless lives and improved the quality of life for many others, with over 233 million people having major surgery a year. That's one in 25. But this wasn't always the case. Surgery without anaesthetic is, obviously, terrifying, but it happened for centuries.

Our earliest evidence of surgery occurring is in Neolithic times, and possibly even earlier. That sentence scares me a bit. Trepanning was the first ever surgery, and possibly one of the worst. It involved creating a hole in the skull to expose dura matter, the bit above the brain. The evidence for trepanning comes from cave paintings depicting the surgery, but the most obvious piece of evidence is skulls with holes in them. This seemed to be a common procedure as well: out of 120 skulls found in a burial site in France, 40 of them had trepanation holes, dating to 6500 BC. There are even skulls dating back to 12000 BC with trepanation holes. Why would people put themselves through this? Most likely because it was believed trepanning could cure diseases, prevent epileptic seizures, cure mental disorders and help with migraines. Obviously, anaesthetic hadn't been invented yet, so this would've been a painful process with about 50% survival rate. I'd have the migraine instead.

The Egyptians were some of the first to branch out from just trepanning, although they did it as well. They're believed to be the first people that carried out circumcisions, although it's unlikely this was for medicinal purposes and is more likely that it was in a ritual when a boy took his first steps into manhood. They would have had the equivalent of a GP conduct this surgery, but had many specialist doctors as well, including proctologists, dentists and gastroenterologists. All of them would have been referred to as "Wabau", meaning someone who knows magic. Doctors could be men or women, and there was even a "Chief of Dentists and Physicians", the earliest dating back to 2700 BC.

Their knowledge of the heart, lungs and vessels carrying air and blood was aided by the Nile. It was understood that if part of the Nile was blocked off, the crops on the banks surrounding the tributary wouldn't grow, and life itself would cease to exist. The same goes for the human body, with each vessel acting as a tributary, carrying nutrients, oxygen, and life to parts of the body. Not only that, but their knowledge of bone structure was surprisingly accurate, as well as knowledge about the brain and the liver.

Not all of it was as sophisticated, however. The Egyptians were quick to blame mental illness, among other things, on evil spirits sent down by the gods. A papyrus from 1600 BC shows that the way to cure mental illness was to engage in recreational activities such as dancing and painting, as well as participating in rituals for the gods. A good treatment for many things often came back to faecal matter from just about any animal they could get their hands on. Fly droppings, cooked mice and cat fat were some remedies, not to mention the first ever birth control: a plug of crocodile dung stuffed up the vagina.

Again, no anaesthetic. Honey was the only thing used during and post-treatment to cover any wounds.

The Ancient Greeks had good doctors too, most notably Hippocrates, the Father of Modern Medicine. Hippocrates lived from 460 BC to 377 BC and shaped the way medicine is done to this day. He believed that the same treatment shouldn't be applied to many different diseases, but each one had a different cause and, therefore, deserved its own treatment. Greek medicine also gave us the *Rod of Asclepius,* the serpent entwined rod symbol that's seen commonly in medicine today.

Greek medicine became more sophisticated and more complex, with one of the main procedures being ligation, a procedure still carried out to this day. Many physicians had their training on dissected animals such as pigs and monkeys, but even dissected criminals… alive. Nerves and vessels became mapped around the body, medicine schools were set up to train physicians, with gods and bad spirits not really being a part of medicine. It was looking up.

The Romans had a strong Greek influence when it came to surgery and medicine as a whole, even constructing temples to the Greek god Apollo, who was believed to have healing powers. But another reason for this strong influence was the fact that many Greek physicians moved to Rome to complete their work, such as Galen, who proposed the theory of Four Humours. This theory stated that health relied on the balance of four humours in the body: blood, yellow bile, black bile and phlegm). He also used people's dreams as a way of diagnosing them, but anyway. Spatulas, forceps, catheters, scalpels and more were designed and became commonplace in hospitals. Surgery became less common as many people died as a result. Herbal treatments were more popular: egg yolk was used to cure dysentery, cooked liver was used to prevent eye soreness, birthwort (poisonous) was used in childbirth and rhubarb was used for flatulence.

The Middle Ages got a bit weird. They carried on using the theory of Four Humours and, therefore, believed that the best way to cure many ailments was to get rid of a lot of blood. The common practice known as bloodletting, a practice used until the 19ᵗʰ century — possibly even later. They called it a *blood-worm*, but we now know it as a leech: a method of getting blood out of the body. It became so common that people would practice bloodletting even if they had nothing wrong with them and did it just to stay healthy. The Middle Ages cure for haemorrhoids is equally as bad. It's worse actually. Haemorrhoids were named Saint Fiacre's Illness, obviously named after Saint Fiacre, patron saint of gardeners, herbalists and sufferers of haemorrhoids. Up until the 12ᵗʰ century, the way to cure haemorrhoids was to use a red-hot iron rod (you see where I'm going with this) and stick it up the anus. This was until Jewish physician Moses Maimonides came along and prescribed a bath instead. Much nicer. Barbers were used as surgeons as they had good skills with scissors and knives, but not as good anatomical knowledge. Urine was used as an antiseptic on battle wounds and eye surgery was relatively common, although not very nice. To cure cataracts, a thick needle was used to push the cornea to the back of the eye, with no anaesthetic, just a cup of red wine. And of course, trepanning was still commonplace.

Finally, in the 18ᵗʰ century, everything became standardised with the help of John Hunter, surgeon to King George III. He made standard, empirical methods to be used on everyone. He used himself as a test subject for many of his experiments, including ones with gonorrhoea and syphilis. Of course, this is extremely unlikely as his theories were disproven years later, but because of his reputation, people accepted it. As described by one of his biographers: "His nature was kindly and generous, though outwardly rude and repelling.", and one of his assistants described him as "warm and impatient, readily provoked, and when irritated, not easily soothed." Not the ideal way to be described, but he did great things for medicine. He even carried out the first artificial insemination. He built up a collection of over 13,000 organs from various different species, yet still stated that surgical procedures should be done as a last resort.

Percival Pott was also a revolutionary, discovering that carcinogens cause cancer. Scrotal cancer was very common in chimney sweepers, who would work all day within the carcinogenic chambers of chimneys. It was so common that chimney sweepers wouldn't even go to the doctor for it, and instead, opted for self-surgery. One of Pott's observations included a man that had a sizeable carcinoma on his scrotum, but Pott noted that "he seized with a split stick and cut off with a razor. He remarked that it was not very painful. He resumed work the following day." This gave me goosebumps. And not in a good way.

At last, anaesthetic. Before this point, opium may have been used, but only on occasion. The 19th century gave rise to chloroform, the first ever anaesthetic, pioneered by John Snow. Yes, winter is coming, but so was pain free surgery. Chloroform was used on Queen Victoria during childbirth, but it wasn't the safest. Muscle relaxants were soon developed, and anaesthetics became the norm during surgery.

Despite surgery being more pain free, there was still a lot of death due to infection. This was because there was no such thing as antiseptic surgery. This was until Hungarian doctor, Ignaz Semmelweis, who tried and tried again to get people to wash their hands. That's basically all he wanted. He tried to get medical students to do it when in the labour ward and went to the Royal Society to express his concern. They rejected it, and said that hand washing before surgery wasn't important even though gloves weren't used.

It took genius Louis Pasteur, creator of the pasteurisation process for milk, and the rabies, cholera and anthrax vaccines, for antiseptic surgery to be discovered and normalised. Pasteur found there were microorganisms that caused sepsis or other infections and suggested three main ways to get rid of them: filtration, exposure to heat or exposure to chemical solutions. He made his own antiseptic methods before and during surgery, and his work was published 50 years later, becoming common for all doctors and surgeons around France and the rest of Europe. The first sterilising equipment was made, using hot steam on equipment after surgery, saving thousands of lives.

By the end of the 19th century, people got very creative. Here, was the start of psychosurgery. Yes, it's as scary as it sounds. We've already encountered the first method of psychosurgery: trepanning. But doctors wanted to find out if surgery could cure anorexia, OCD, depression and more with a knife in the brain. The whole concept of psychosurgery is based on the fact that everything is in the brain, including mental illnesses. If connections relating to the mental illness were disturbed, then would it be possible to cure them?

Gottleib Burckhardt was the first who wanted to know. As the superintendent at a psychiatric hospital, he was basically allowed to do whatever he wanted, so he operated on six of his patient's brains. Despite many physicians being extremely against Burckhardt's work, it was the precursor to the lobotomy: one of the most infamous medical procedures in history. After a lobotomy, there were obvious complications, with people vomiting, not being able to move their eyes, moving their eyes too much, being incapacitated and ultimately brain damaged. Despite this, 40,000 people in the US were lobotomised, and 17,000 in the UK.

One type of lobotomy is the transorbital lobotomy, which was originally called the ice pick lobotomy. It involved going through the eye socket to reach the brain and make incisions. A hammer of sorts was used with an instrument that looks like an ice pick to go behind the eyes and get into the brain. AAAH. Hundreds of people died from it as a result, with only a few having successful results.

One notable person who had a lobotomy was Rosemary Kennedy, the sister of President John F. Kennedy. She suffered from seizures and mood swings, causing her father to arrange a prefrontal lobotomy for her when she was 23. She was awake during the surgery, with doctors asking her to perform various tasks, such as singing the national anthem or counting backwards. They made a judgement on how far to cut based on how well she responded. As a result of the surgery, Rosemary was instantly institutionalised as doctors said she had the mental capacity of a two-year-old. She was unable to walk or speak, but the Kennedy family weren't allowed to speak out about her or her illness as they did not want to disrupt JFK's run for presidency. It only became common knowledge in 1987. The doctor that performed the surgery, Walter Freeman, was banned from practising surgery after one of his patients suffered a cerebral haemorrhage and died as a result, although as many as 15% of his patients are known to have died during his procedures.

Surgery is no longer a last resort, as it's mostly safe and as clean as you like.

I know this chapter is long, but I found it bloody interesting (no pun intended) and had so much fin writing it.

Other facts that didn't make the cut:

- Some people think Leonardo da Vinci dissected human bodies to make his drawings more accurate.
- Women make up one-third of general surgeons.
- A neurosurgeon's average salary in the US is over $660,000.
- The first male-to-female sex change was done by Sir Harold Gillies in New Zealand, in 1951.
- South Korea has the most people that have undergone plastic surgery per capita.
- The first surgical mask used in surgery was in 1897.
- One in 1,000 patients wake up during surgery.
- The first liposuction was in 1977 in France.
- A rotationplasty is a procedure that turns an ankle into a knee.
- Osteo-odonto-keratoprosthetics helps restore sight using teeth.
- A hemispherectomy is when half of the brain is removed.
- A head transplant takes 36 hours to complete, and over 150 surgeons and nurses.
- Some medical professions include sex surrogate, egg-broker, sleep technologist and flavourist.
- There was an instrument that tightened around cysts to cut off blood flow. Doctors would then just wait for the cyst to fall off. They also used it for haemorrhoids.
- Bee stings are used for arthritis.

Poem about surgery:

Some call me a hypochondriac,

But I don't think I am.

I just go to the doctors after a snack

or maybe after some jam.

That stuff can do real damage,

that's what people don't know.

Especially the likes of cabbage,

because inside you, it grows.

"Doctor, doctor! Please help me!

I have a graze on my knee!"

I get told to shut up,

and get told this frequently.

I look up my symptoms on WebMD

and all that I can find,

I have cancer in my left knee

and in my behind.

So no, I'm not a hypochondriac,

I'm just safe.

It's not long until I go back,

because now, I've got chafe.

16
CHESS

Thank the Pope for Beth Harmon.

Chess is, without a doubt, one of the biggest games in the world, with 605 million adults playing it regularly. That's almost 10% of the entire population of the world. The entire population on this planted. 10%. I don't know; to me, it seems mental for one game to dominate as much of the globe as it does.

If you know the rules of chess, skip this paragraph, because this will be the shortest (but also most comprehensive) introduction to chess you'll ever get: there are two players on an 8x8 board, one being black and the other white. There are six different types of piece: king, queen, bishop, knight, rook and pawn. The queen can move as many moves as she likes diagonally and in straight lines. The bishop can only move diagonally. The knight can move one up and two to the side, or vice versa. Pawns can only move one square up, unless it's the first time they're being moved, when they can move two. The aim is to "checkmate" the other player's king — a piece that can only move one square in any direction. Checkmate means that their king is currently under attack and can't to move to a safe square. If the king is being threatened but can still move safely, that's just known as "check". If a player has no available moves but isn't in check, it's known as a "stalemate", which is a draw. Phew.

It all started in the year 600 in India, when chess was first played. It was called *chaturanga* (a fantastic name might I add), translating as "four divisions". It was called this because of the major pieces on the board (besides the queen): the infantry (now the pawn), cavalry (knight), elephantry (bishop) and chariot (rook). The Muslim traders introduced the game to the Persians, who absolutely loved it. They got very into it as well, exclaiming "Shah!", meaning "King!", when the player attacked the king, and shouting "Shah Mat!" when their king couldn't move. Say shah mat out loud. Sound familiar?

Indians used chaturanga not only as a game but also for military strategy, mathematics and gambling due to its strategic nature, finding patterns, and being generally difficult. Although, they had some rules different to what we do now:

- The queen, now the most agile piece on the board, was able to move one square diagonally *only*.
- The bishop, or as it was known then, the *elephant*, moved one square diagonally and one square forward, supposedly like the legs of an elephant.
- In other versions, the elephant could move two squares diagonally *and* jump a piece.
- A stalemated player was the winner.
- A stalemated player could take one of their enemy's pieces that'd still have the king in check.

Chess remained largely the same and seemed to just pop up in many places, meaning pieces acquired some funny names. In Mongolia, the king, queen, bishop, horse, cart and pawn were called *lord, dog* (because she was protector of the livestock, not sexist), *camel, horse, cart* and *boy* respectively.

By the 11th and 12th centuries, there was a strong link between social value and chess. Chess was seen as a prestigious pastime, with only those of high nobility and high culture playing it. Chess boards became very, very expensive with intricate designs made of various different materials. Queen Margaret of England had a very expensive chess set and her green and red chess board and pieces were made of jasper and crystal. With the lesser vying for such nobility, chess became unbelievably popular. So popular that that in England, it was decided there needed to be a patron. So, King Henry I, King Henry II and Richard the Lionheart were all chess patrons, and Ivan the Terrible gaining a similar status in Russia. By 1234, chess was so popular that in France, King Louis IX had to issue an ordinance against gambling as people were gambling on matches — a sinful thing to do.

Two hundred years later, the queen and the bishop had had enough crap from everyone and decided they wanted to be a good piece. The bishop wanted to move diagonally for as many squares as it pleased, and the queen to move both in straight lines *and* diagonally for as many moves as she desired. This chess became known as *Queen's Chess* and is the same chess we play to this day.

People loved this new chess even more than the last one. Chess clubs became common in the 19th century, chess boards were in most coffee houses and, by the 19th century, chess problems were common, in the same way sudoku is now.

An obvious issue started to arise in the 1851 London Chess Tournament. One player took over two and a half hours to make a single move. The game was just taking far too long. There were two solutions: completely ignore the fact that the game was taking too long and adjourn the match if a player needs sleep or gets hungry, or add time limits. Adjourning was difficult as the player who moved last would be at a disadvantage as the other player would have a long time, overnight perhaps, to think about their next move. So, the *sealed move* was created, by which the player to move last before adjournment would tell the referee the next move, write it down, and seal it in an envelope without the other player knowing what that move is. The simple solution, however, was time limits. Time limits were used for the first time in 1861, first with sandglasses and later, pendulums. Much easier.

Both World Wars happened, but that didn't stop anyone playing chess, most notably the Soviets who dominated the chess world (insert a joke about the Soviets dominating the world here). This was until American Bobby Fischer was born and played the best chess anyone had ever seen. Starting playing chess at the age of six, Fischer's knowledge of chess and his unbelievable IQ was nothing like anyone had ever seen before. At the age of 14, Fischer was the youngest ever US champion and at 15, he became the youngest grandmaster ever. He dropped out of school at 16 saying, "you don't learn anything at school". At 20, Fischer won the 1972 World Chess Championship, meaning he was set to play Boris Spassky of the USSR. An immense amount of pressure was placed on Fischer's shoulders, as an American vs a Soviet in chess represented so much more than just that. It was dubbed "The Match of the Century" and received front-page media coverage not only in the US, but also the rest of the world. Despite the pressure, Fischer went on to win the title, becoming world champion. Although Fischer played for a while after this match, he stopped playing at his peak. But his story doesn't stop there.

Fischer's mother was Jewish, but he hated the religion. His first antisemitic comments were heard in the 1960s, with people saying he even idolised Hitler and all he stood for. Fischer believed the Jewish controlled the US and he became relentlessly involved in every conspiracy under the sun. He fled the US and lived in various countries from 1992 to 2002, including Hungary and the Philippines. The US

Chess Federation had to revoke his membership when he said that he supported the 9/11 attacks in the US.

Fischer was in Japan, flying back to the Philippines, when he was arrested after being tipped off by the US Government for using an invalid passport. He resisted arrest, suffering bruises and a broken tooth and was deported. He lived in Iceland under an alien passport until his death. It's widely speculated that that he had schizophrenia, developing similar fears similar to those of Adolf Hitler — a man also thought to have schizophrenia.

World Chess Champion Gary Kasparov was also regarded as one of the greats in chess. He has also had an interesting chess and post-chess career. He was ranked number one in the world for 255 months, losing to the great match against the IBM computer *Deep Blue*. This was a pivotal moment, not only for chess but for technology, as it showed that a computer's intellect was greater than that of a human. Despite it being a computer, Kasparov still accused it of cheating. After chess, Kasparov took part in many civil rights rallies in Russia, even stating that he was going to run for President of Russia. In 2013, he announced that he'd fled for Croatia for fear of prosecution under the lead of Vladimir Putin. Oh, what a different place the world would be if he'd won.

Since then, chess has stayed the same. Besides one rule which states that if a player has any electrical equipment, including a mobile phone, that generates noise during a match, they forfeit. But that's it.

Other facts that didn't make the cut:

- The longest game of chess, theoretically, is 5,949 moves.
- The longest official chess game was 269 moves long.
- The number of possible chess games is greater than the number of electrons in the universe. There are just over 10000000000000000000000000000000000000000 00000000000000000000000000000000000000000 00000000000000000000000000000000000000 possible chess games.
- The second book ever written in English was about chess.
- The oldest chess set still around dates back to the 12th century and was used in the making of the film of Harry Potter and the Philosopher's stone.
- Armenia has the highest number of grandmasters per capita in the world.
- Russia and Armenia have chess as part of their school curriculum.
- A Turk by the name of Wolfgang von Kempelen created an "automatic chess machine". The machine beat Napoleon Bonaparte. The machine contained a chess master playing the opposite pieces on the inside.
- Chess Boxing is a sport where athletes box, then play chess, then box etc. until one of them is knocked out, or checkmate is achieved.
- Playing one and a half hours of chess per week will burn 0.08kg per month.
- During an intense chess competition, competitors will burn 6,000 calories a day. This is due to elevated heart rates, increased breathing rates and immense concentration.

Poem about chess:

Where, where do I put my queen?

e4, or e5 looks pretty clean.

Check, no, maybe, checkmate!

Have I found it? Is it too late?

Where, where do I put my rook.

Oh dear, look how much time I took

Maybe he won't see my tick,

If I put it here, on f6.

Where, where do I put my bishop?

I think I'll have to redevelop.

Aah, maybe he won't see my fork.

This dude isn't good. What a dork.

Uh oh.

Where, where do I put my king?

It's not over until the fat lady sings.

But I think he's got me; I think he's done it.

He screams "checkmate". I quit.

THE HISTORY OF SOME STUFF

17
TAMPONS

There's no doubt that with me being male, this book was, and is at risk of becoming too male dominated — perhaps not appealing to a larger audience. So, without further ado, the history of tampons.

It's a topic that's still taboo to this day, although I'd like to think I'm part of the process of taking down the stigma by educating more people about tampons and the history of them. Women have been having periods since the dawn of time, meaning that there had to be ways to stay clean and hygienic. Throughout history, there have been some strange things put into vaginas to aid menstrual flow, as well as contraception.

The Egyptians were the first to come up with the idea of plugging using pessaries (defined as "*a small soluble block that is inserted into the vagina to treat infection or as a contraceptive*" by the OED). As mentioned before, crocodile dung was also used as contraception, but there are some other methods were used, too. These include getting earth from the Nile banks, crushing it up with honey and galena (a lead sulphide mineral), getting a wad of linen to wrap it in and leaving it inside the vagina. 0-1 to infections.

It's a possibility that Hippocrates, the Father of Modern Medicine, also spoke about tampons and how women should use them. He said that women should use a material such as lint to wrap around a stick and insert it when necessary. Although it's unlikely that this was used to stop menstrual flow, there's some evidence to suggest that people used it as contraception, although I'm not entirely sure how that'd work.

700 years after Hippocrates in India, there were various Sanskrit texts to suggest that tampons were recommended to women. But not exactly the-height-of-luxury-tampons. They were made out of oil and salt. A very effective contraceptive, as the rock salt would kill all the sperm. But again, not exactly a tampon, and it probably hurt like a bitch.

Another possibility: the Japanese used rolls of paper held in place by a bandage called a *kama*. But paper, especially over a thousand years ago, didn't have the most absorbent properties in the world, so this tampon had to be changed over 12 times a day. Not ideal.

With the Middle Ages, did a brand-new invention arrive to help women through menstruation and let them lead normal lives? No. Unfortunately not. Although, the reasons may be justified. Many people had very poor nutrition, meaning many were anaemic and had very low body fat with not many nutrients. This would mean that periods were often irregular, further apart and, in some cases, non-existent. We can see this happening today in those suffering from malnutrition or in long-distance runners. Moreover, women were having children and breastfeeding at a much earlier age to what women are now. As breastfeeding encourages earlier menopause, women over the age of 30 weren't going to have any more periods, so the demand part of supply and demand just wasn't there.

Obviously, periods still existed, and it was an issue for those who experienced them. When in a situation that required a tampon-like product, medieval women were forced to make their own and many women chose to use scrap fabrics, usually made out of cotton. Although an expensive material, it was chosen over the likes of wool because it was more absorbent and less scratchy. For those unable to afford cotton, they'd use anything they could find. Wool was a cheap alternative, but a very uncomfortable one. Women would wear special underwear to keep these makeshift pads in place, but some women opted for a tampon similar to that of Hippocrates' solution. Women would, again, use cotton or wool depending on their wealth, find a twig or rod, wrap the cloth around it and insert. It's possible women used various plants as well. There's a plant, a type of bog moss, used to soak up the blood of soldiers on the battlefield. Seeing this, women may have used this as a cotton replacement. Various etymologists believe this is why the moss is called *blood moss*.

But now, it's 12 September 1933 and Earle Haas patented the first ever tampon and sold it to the general public, marketed as "Tampax".

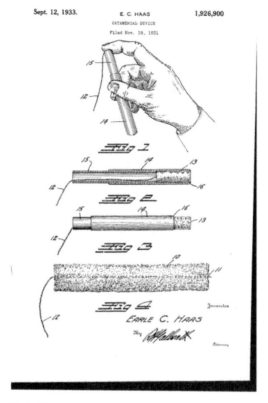

Earle Haas' tampon patent.

They were an instant hit with the help of clever marketing and advertisement. They had their place in the Second World War as well when tampons were mass produced, as the they'd soak up blood from wounds and gunshots and prevent infection.

Since then, the tampon hasn't really changed, but there's still a way to go. The tampon tax is in place in many countries around the world, branding the tampon as a luxury item, which it obviously isn't. Women in prison have to make their own tampons out of toilet paper if needed, increasing the risk of toxic shock syndrome, and many homeless women are still unable to afford them. Go sign a petition.

Other facts that didn't make the cut:

- The average woman spends $1,733 on tampons each year.
- The average woman uses 11,400 tampons throughout her life, if tampons are the only period products used.
- Tampons have a shelf life of around five years.
- The word *tampon* is derived from the word "tampion" in French, meaning plug.
- The number of droplets on a tampon box shows how absorbent they are. Four droplets is *super* absorbent.
- Many tampons are tested by being inserted into condoms.
- China is the largest consumer of tampons.
- The feminine hygiene market is predicted to be worth USD 53 billion by 2023.
- Religious leaders in the 1940s believed that inserting a tampon would cause sexual arousal in women.
- Tampons have been used as makeshift contraception, as they can block the entrance to the cervix. This is not recommended.
- The first scented tampon was made in 1971 by Playtex — the same company that made Neil Armstrong's space suit.
- The first Anti-Tampon Conference was held in 2000.
- The first tampons in space arrived in 1983, with American Sally Rider.

Poem about tampons:

Tampons are great.

There's no need for hate,

but let's get this straight:

women pay more coming out the gate,

because of tax unless you're extremely lightweight.

Periods are innate,

there's no debate.

You could be eight

or thirty-eight.

The rule still relates.

Time for an update.

18
DOORS

Again, you may ask "Why doors? This is really random."
You'd be correct.

~~We all think of doors as~~ We don't think of doors.
They're always sort of just… there. The only time we think
of them is if a new house is being built and you think "Shit,
we've forgotten about a new door", or if you hit your head.
I'm here to change that. This is a whole chapter about doors,
and it's more interesting than it sounds, with some of the
most genuinely beautiful sculptures and artwork I've ever
seen.

The first door in the whole of human history was over
4000 years ago, circa the 20th century BC. No one knows
exactly who invented this door, but of course, it was the
Egyptians. This wasn't a door for any human, or any animal
for that matter. This was a door for the spirit. In tombs, the
Egyptians would paint and carve what is now called a *false*

door. It was a place where the soul of the deceased could escape and go into the afterlife. Family members would put offerings at this door so that the spirit could quickly come grab the offering, and then travel back to the land of the dead.

Egypt was, and still is, immensely dry and a very hot climate, so doors were needed in order to retain some moisture and coolth during the hot seasons. Amazingly, the doors in Ancient Egypt were hinged: the first hinged doors in history. Many were made from wood, such as the olive wood mentioned in the Bible. King Solomon's temple, the *First Temple*, is said to have had olive wood doors, carved with intricate detailing and overlaid with gold. Why not choose this as your new front door?

Some of the biggest doors of their time were the Gates of Balawat (called gates but are doors, trust me), huge doors that stood 8.2 meters tall, encased in bronze and embossed with decorative figures at war. Although not hinged, these huge doors are opened by turning equally huge pine pillars, also decorated with bronze, in their own stone sockets. These doors from 2800 years ago provided us with a narrative of what happened with the Assyrian Kings from 800 BC to 600 BC, as their art stretched over 285 feet long when put in a line and are one of the few items from the Neo-Assyrian Empire to tell a story of the empire, telling us today what technological advances they'd made, how their people worked, how they conducted war and more. Who knew you could get so much from a door?

The Romans were very weird with their doors. The doors themselves had nothing wrong with them, but it was how they conducted themselves with doors and a door's place in society. Romans had their own god for doors, Janus, who presided over the beginning and end of conflict and, therefore, war and peace. The doors of Rome were opened during war and closed during peace to honour Janus. The doors were open a lot. Doors had a very symbolic meaning and message in Roman times, as Janus was also the god of beginnings and endings; you could walk through a door and literally meet your end.

The Greeks and Romans invented some fantastic doors, including sliding doors, folding doors, even automatic doors in the 1st century AD. Heron, a man living in Alexandria, was extremely good at maths and understood how the world worked like few had ever done before. He used all his knowledge to make the automatic door.

It's actually quite cool.

He used his own hydraulic system to open and close doors and called his invention *Machine 37*. It was used by priests and congregations in temples so that the doors would open as if by magic. A priest would walk up to the doors, rather theatrically might I add, and light a fire on a pit, which had some secrets underneath. This wouldn't be enough on its own; sacrifices were needed to fuel the fire. The heat from the fire would cause water to be displaced, moving it, using its weight to move the doors. They'd slowly creep open, as if to say the gods were happy and pleased with the sacrifice made. Not only this, but compressed air from this mechanism would be pushed through trumpet-like instruments, creating an immense cacophony. This was, and still is, an amazing feat of engineering.

Medieval doors in the west are usually made with vertical planks of wood, backed with either horizontal planks or diagonal bracing, and strengthened with those long iron hinges and iron nails that are so stereotypical of medieval doors. Doors in the medieval era were commonly quite small; it's a misconception that people back then had small doors because they were small. It is true that people were smaller, but not that much smaller. It's more probable that the doors were smaller because of the expensive materials needed. This meant that doors, especially large doors, were very expensive, so having a small door was just good sense. Rather duck every time you leave home than spend all your savings.

Post-Middle Ages, the Renaissance came, and it came

with a heap of wealth — but only for the wealthy. Having great doors was a statement of your wealth and nobility to anyone that came to your home. Unsurprisingly, during this time, it was the French that had large, elaborate, decorative doors, with Louis XIV and Louis XV having columns and entablatures beside doors of their palaces. Even the poorer wanted a greater status and used any material they could get their hands on, usually copper or bronze, to make decorations for their doors.

Craftsmanship for door-making peaked during the Renaissance, with techniques from Michelangelo and Da Vinci being used all over the world to decorate doors. As religion reigned supreme, many of the cathedral doors were covered in Gothic decorations, even having motifs. I want my door to have a motif.

Skip forward about four centuries, taking us to 1963, when NASA had a big problem. NASA needed to have a building big enough to assemble rockets and get them out. This big problem required a big solution. They settled on building the VAB, standing for Vehicle Assemble Building, which is one of the most voluminous building in the world, measuring 3,665,000 m^3. That's over three times the space of the Empire State Building squished into one. It's so big that it even has its own weather; on humid days, it's said that rain clouds form at the top of the building. What the heck.

Anyways.

The VAB needed a way to get out its equipment to go to space for the Apollo program. So, they built the biggest door in the world. Standing 139 meters high, these doors are so immense that they take 45 minutes to open completely, and another 45 to close completely. Bit of an inconvenience having to wait in your rocket for 45 minutes for some doors to open.

That's it really for doors; they haven't changed a whole lot, unless you were uber wealthy and French and a king and lived in the Renaissance.

Other facts that didn't make the cut:

- The band "The Doors" got their name from the Aldous Huxley book *"The Doors of Perception"*.
- Insufficiently glazed doors and windows amount to a 25% increase in energy bills.
- The oldest doors in England are the ones in Westminster Abbey, dating from 1050.
- The last monarch to go through the doors of the House of Commons was Charles I in 1642.
- Feng Shui dictates you should have an open, clear pathway to the door to support a harmonious flow of energy throughout the house.
- Some Romans decorated their doors with large phalluses.
- One-third of burglars enter through a house's front door.
- According to some oneirologists, dreaming about doors either means either there's a new opening in your life (if it's open), or a missed opportunity (if it's closed).
- New York City law dictates that revolving doors cannot complete more than 15 revolutions in one minute, as it'd be too dangerous for the people inside.
- The Cheyenne Mountain Complex in Colorado Springs has 25-tonne doors that can withstand a 30-megaton blast. That's 1,429 Nagasaki "Fat Mans".
- The door to the President of Colombia looks like wood, but is made from steel: bulletproof, fireproof and with a biometric system to detect whether blood is flowing through the person (to check that they are alive).

Poem about doors:

Oh, what can you do to me?

Can you open up or make me bleed?

I've been banging here for hours

As I have lost my keys.

Oh, can you open up?

Please don't make me pee in a cup.

I don't mean to be rude but,

It's my body I don't want to interrupt!

Oh, please can I come inside?

I don't want to leave you dissatisfied

by not opening up.

Some oil, can I prescribe?

Oh, this won't work.

I don't need your handiwork.

Just a locksmith to get me in.

Who knew doors could be such jerks.

19
COMEDY

A chapter on comedy needs no introduction. If it does, I prescribe two hours of either Friends or The Office (US or UK), twice a week. If that doesn't work, you're a lost cause.

It's no secret that the Greeks were extremely theatrical, as shown by the immensity of the buildings, the fine white marble used throughout society, gold and silver everywhere and of course, theatres. Greek tragedy was big, but so was comedy, although I'm not sure we'd find it all that funny today.

Comedy in Greece can be split into three parts, all very creatively named: Old Comedy, Middle Comedy and New Comedy. Wow.

Old Comedy was a precursor to middle comedy and was underdeveloped and not as popular as Middle Comedy. Old Comedy consisted of poets and dramatists, such as Aristophanes, drawing on political satire and innuendoes about sex and poo. Seems the Greeks were as immature as we are now. Plays contained buffoonish caricatures of figures in history, such as the portrayal of Socrates in *The Clouds*, by Aristophanes. The chorus had a major influence on the plot, and of course, the stereotypical Greek masks were used. These are huge overhead masks that have exaggerated expressions so that people far away could see the character and what they were thinking and to convey characters with predictable physical traits.

Little is known about Middle Comedy as no plays have stood the test of time, but we do know that the chorus had no influence on the plot and there were some stock characters, such as the conceited cook, boastful soldiers, parasites, philosophers and courtesans.

New Comedy is where comedy really thrived though. Following the death of Alexander the Great in 332 BC, New Comedy was born and lasted for 90 years in Ancient Greece. It strayed away from political satire and focused more on the everyday, comparable to what's known as *situation comedy* today. Everything became less grotesque and more in line with what was socially acceptable. There were stock characters just as before: the permissive father figure, the stern father, kind prostitutes and cunning servants. Writers and poets of New Comedy were viewed as famous in society and had great nobility. This status came with perks of course, one of them being having access to the "high-tier" prostitutes of society. Good reason to become a comic I suppose.

Roman comedy was largely derived from Greek comedy, although it seems we know a little more about it due to a higher number of surviving plays. One of the famous Roman playwrights was Plautus, who used poetic meters and was admired for his depth of comedy. Most Roman comedies contained the same stock characters:

- *adelescens* – the unmarried man in his late twenties who's in love with a prostitute and, therefore, cannot marry, but it turns out in the end that she's actually free and, therefore, can marry.
- *senex* – father to the *adelescens* who's concerned with

his relationship with his son. He opposes his son's love choice but goes along with it. He also tries to get women but is caught by the angry wife. Tut tut senex.

- *leno* – a modern-day pimp, using his slaves for wealth.
- *miles gloriosus* – an arrogant soldier (sound familiar?).
- *parasitus* – a selfish liar.
- *matrona* – the wife and mother, always getting in the way of the *senex* and his will for other women.
- *virgo* – the love interest of the *adelescens* but often not present on stage and is rather just spoken of.

You see? Very similar to the Greek.

By the Elizabethan era, comedy had taken on a different meaning. Shakespeare had a pretty big say in what goes, and he said that a comedy is one with a happy ended and is more light-hearted than other plays. It didn't even have to be funny. For example, I wouldn't call *A Midsummer Night's Dream* hilarious, but it's a comedy, nonetheless.

1662 was a big year for comedy in Britain. The one and only *Punch and Judy* made its first appearance and people loved it. The outrageousness provoked shocked laughter that hadn't been seen since Old Comedy 2000 years prior. Punch and Judy could be updated with new hand puppets, meaning political satire was making a comeback. Punch and Judy became the spirit of the nation.

Pantomimes were the next big hit and have been around since the 1800s. Slapstick comedy was involved and people loved it just as much as Punch and Judy. Joseph Grimaldi participated in many of these pantomimes, performing as "Joey" the clown. The stages of the pantomime provided a platform for Stan Laurel and Oliver Hardy, Charlie Chaplain and others, meaning comedy was becoming more and more mainstream and accessible.

Joey the clown, looking very funny and not scary at all.

Surreal humour was the next big thing, that being things that just don't make sense. People found it incredibly amusing. *Alice's Adventures in Wonderland* is an example, featuring a smoking caterpillar, croquet matches with flamingos and a time-keeping waistcoat-wearing bunny.

The 20th century was a notable century for many things — and comedy was one of them. The television meant that people such as Laurel and Hardy, Charlie Chaplain and Marcel Marceau could move from the stage to the big screen. And they did. Radio and TV meant that comedy was everywhere where it had been inaccessible before, allowing the mid-20th century to give rise to names such as Robin

Williams, Eddie Murphy, Joan Rivers… the list goes on. Stand-up comedy was becoming popular as well, giving small-time comedians to have a place on stage to be funny and, if they were lucky, have an agent come up to them at the end of a show and offer them another gig.

Comedy was diversifying and developed more and more sub-genres. *The Simpsons, M*A*S*H, The Office, Blackadder*: all these shows that have shaped so many childhoods and lives, helping people through the hardest of times.

I think that's why comedy has survived so long; it helps people escape into a joyous place and forget the worries in their lives. It has such immense power to change people's moods and make them feel better. It's something we definitely take for granted.

Other facts that didn't make the cut:

- The top three highest grossing comedies are kids' movies: *Toy Story 3*, *Frozen*, *and The Lion King*. All great films too.
- One comedy in 1997 was named *Trojan War* and had a budget of $15 million. It amassed $309 at the box office.
- Bob Newhart's real name is George.
- Tyra Banks wanted to be a comedian before she was scouted.
- Johnny Depp, Tom Cruise and Jim Carrey were all considered for the role of Ferris Bueller.
- *The Tonight Show* is the oldest talk show in the world.
- Speaking of… Jimmy Fallon was voted "Most Likely to Replace David Letterman" in high school.
- Kevin Hart used the pseudonym "Lil Kev" for his first gig.
- John Cleese has auctioned off a piece of his colon.
- Mike Meyers was offered the role of *Shrek* at the premiere of *Saving Private Ryan*. Very similar movies when you think about it.
- John Krasinski initially went to *The Office* audition for Dwight but changed the producer's mind who let him audition as Jim.
- *Friends* was originally called *Insomnia Café*. Scary.
- By the final season of *Friends*, each actor was earning $1 million per episode.
- Bruce Willis lost a bet with Matthew Perry. That's the only reason he's in *Friends*.

Poem about comedy:

Ha ha. Very funny.

But not too much,

It hurts my tummy.

Oh, look, now I'm crying,

People might say

it looks like I'm dying.

Oh, no. Maybe I am.

I cannot breathe,

my throat is jammed.

Oh, no, this can't be it.

I'm dying from a TV show

which is a bit shit.

Oh my gosh it hurts my spleen.

Maybe next time,

I won't watch Mr Bean.

20
HOUSEPLANTS

This chapter is dedicated to my mother, who has recently gone plant-crazy.

What better way to finish off a book than with houseplants. I have seven plants in my bedroom and they're supposed to make me more productive. I'm not sure if they do, but I know they're trying their best.

Our first piece of evidence for houseplants comes from ancient China circa the 10th century BC, where potted plants were the norm. Due to the climate, plants could be grown with ease in houses as well as outside. Although people may have grown houseplants to make homemade remedies when someone was ill, there's evidence to suggest that the ancient Chinese had their very own garden shows, exhibiting the plants in a decorative manner to show off to everyone else.

Around 400 years later in the 6th century BC, Neo-Babylonian ruler King Nebuchadnezzars II (at least half of you skipped over that word and the other half read it out in your head syllable by syllable) built the *Hanging Gardens of*

Babylon. Supposedly, he built it for his wife, Queen Amytis, who missed the greenery and the rolling hills of her homeland, Medes. This enormous structure was so unbelievably beautifully decorated, with its pristine marble columns, waterfalls flowing from one floor to another and of course, plants everywhere. Plum trees, date trees, palm trees, Ficus — all the plants you could get in the Neo-Babylonian Empire, they were there. Now, technically, we don't know much about this. In fact, we don't know if it even existed. But if it did, it would've acted as a second home to Queen Amydis and, therefore, all the plants would've been houseplants. I cannot recommend looking up photos of the Hanging Gardens of Babylon enough, especially when you recognise that all of it was done over 2,000 years ago.

A depiction of the *Hanging Gardens of Babylon*

Houseplants came to a bit of a halt until the 15th century, although kitchen gardens were common in the medieval era. People were able to grow plants such as onions, leeks, radishes, peas etc. A common flower to have in one's house was the gillyflower, commonly known as the carnation. This was also a common flower in Chinese weddings and is the national flower of Spain. It's one of the first flowers that people had in their houses as decoration.

However, the Renaissance was the time where plant collecting became rather fashionable. Collectors in Italy, the Netherlands and Belgium imported plants all the way from Asia and the East Indies to add life to places where there was little before. People in the 17th century realised you could breed your own plants, meaning there were new species being made and people could collect their own exotic plants easier than ever. By the 18th century, Europe was home to citrus, jasmine, aloes and agaves — all native to the likes of Oceania and Asia.

As the Victorian era drew in, the middle class were at the social struggle of the millennium, with everyone vying for a greater social status. One of the ways to boost their status (in addition to all the others mentioned in the book) was with houseplants from exotic lands. The first ever terrariums were made and shown in houses, decorating drawing rooms with their greenery and life. Drawing rooms of the Victorian era are often shown as dark and smoky places, but it's possible there was an abundance of greenery as decoration.

Early 20th century meant that ceiling-to-floor windows were being used by the rich, creating a seamless transition between the inside and out, aided of course by the plants that decorated the interior. It seems that houseplants were on the rise. This was until war struck.

War inflicted everywhere around the globe during WWII, meaning houseplants were put on hold. Fair enough. When the war finally ended in 1945, people partied like never before, and for some reason, plants made a huge comeback. They were a cheap and easy way of brightening up a room and if you bought a cactus, they were very easy to take care of. As manufacturing developed, plants became easier to take care of and you could now find directions on how to plant plants. Woohoo! Plants such as spider plants, Ficus, orchids, and succulents became common, and that's where we are today.

Most people have plants in their house; maybe it's because of Feng Shui. But nonetheless, houseplants are definitely becoming more common, and are a great way to decorate. So, if this chapter hasn't inspired you to go and buy a houseplant, here's your sign to go get one. It might not change your life, but it'll do its very best to improve it.

Other facts that didn't make the cut:

- Having plants in an office reduces stress.
- It takes 15 spider plants to purify the air of an average house.
- Plants can even reduce noise pollution.
- The oldest pot plant in the world was planted in 1775 in South Africa, and now lives in the Royal Botanical Gardens, UK.
- The world's smelliest plant, the *Amorphophallus titanum* smells like rotten flesh, and also has the world's largest bloom.
- The world's biggest tree is a giant sequoia, measuring 275ft, or 83 meters tall. Bloody heck.
- The oldest tree in the world dates back to the 3rd millennium BC and is called the Great Basin Bristlecone Pine.
- You can eat the seeds of a money plant after they've been roasted.
- The top three most popular house plants are the Fiddle Leaf Fig, the Chinese Money Plant and the Spider Plant.
- Air plants use their roots for attachment to other things, not for absorbing nutrients.
- The *Monstera deliciosa* produces delicious fruit that tastes like a combination of pineapple and strawberry.
- Common names for the *Monstera deliciosa* include Swiss Cheese Plant, Monster Plant, Fruit Salad Plant and Mexican Breadfruit.
- Cacti can live for 200 years.
- According to www.konnecthq.com, "cacti can be very big or very small". Riveting.
- My cactus is called Steve.

Poem about houseplants:

Oh, Steve what are you doing to me?

I'm trying to water you, but you're too spiky.

I have to do it once a week,

But it's too much. I can't take your cheek.

Oh, Steve will you ever flower?

I feel like I've been staring for hours and hours.

Maybe I've given you too much water,

and maybe it's time for me to slaughter.

Oh, Steve, what a great day!

You've flowered! What can I say...

I have the greenest thumbs of all around.

Pay me for my services... five pounds.

Fin.

THE HISTORY OF SOME STUFF

ABOUT THE AUTHOR

Okay, so there's nothing stopping the author from writing this bit of the book. So here I am, writing an unbiased *About the Author* section.

Ethan Cox is a self-published Danish-South-African-English author born in 2003 who has major six-pack abs, even when he doesn't do any exercise, and eats a family bag of crisps every day. He bloody loves tea, and can handle his drink, being able to drink more than Andre the Giant. Although his friends thought his coffee addiction was bad when he was 14, look where he is now. He has a cactus called Steve. Ethan is 6ft 2in, taller than his dad.

Printed in Great Britain
by Amazon

58995376R00092